D1556976

Uncommon Profits through
Stock Purchase Warrants

Uncommon Profits through Stock Purchase Warrants

S. LAWRENCE PRENDERGAST

 1973

DOW JONES-IRWIN, INC   Homewood, Illinois 60430

First Printing, April 1973

ISBN 0-87094-052-X

Library of Congress Catalog Card No. 72–96527

Printed in the United States of America

For my parents,
Marjorie and Edward Stephen Prendergast

Preface

COMMON STOCK purchase warrants are at once the most speculative and the most mysterious of all corporate security instruments. The typical investor, one who manages. his own portfolio, views warrants as the private realm of "professionals." He has been told that warrants are highly complicated devices, issued only by floundering firms, and bought only by the shrewd professional, never by the investing public. He avoids warrants in the same way that he shuns commodity futures contracts, other options, and currency hedges. Warrants, unlike these other speculations, have the additional attribute of being born and bred from despair. The failure of investment trusts in the 1930s and the subsequent reorganizations resulted in many warrant issues that performed poorly, perpetuating the gloom and identifying warrants with the period and its problems. Consequently, there is a great lack of understanding about the instrument. This lack of understanding continues because of the quality and quantity of information available concerning warrants. There is but a small body of literature on the subject. Significant writings have occurred only in the last twenty years. Most of these have appeared in private publications which are generally unknown and unavailable to the public. Go to the finest business library in the land, consult the card catalog, and you will find only one or two references to stock purchase warrants. Articles that do appear in leading and widely read periodicals generally present a superficial analysis of currently available warrants. This book provides a bibliography of all relevant writings to date. It is hoped that the reader, having developed a genuine interest in the subject, will consult some of the referenced works.

It is the purpose of this book to dispel the myths of warrants and to equip the individual investor with the tools needed to analyze and utilize common stock purchase warrants effectively. First, rest assured that warrants are not mysterious, are not relegated to professionals, are not evil, and are not beyond the scope and portfolio of the investing public. Anyone who takes it upon himself to manage his own portfolio should be able to evaluate this market instrument. The warrant is to the investor what the level is to the carpenter; that is, just another tool, but one which helps him do the job expertly. As the carpenter knows and utilizes the tools in his box, you should understand and make use of the market vehicles at your disposal. Warrants may not have a place in your portfolio, at a given time or ever, but that utilization or lack of it should be the result of careful analysis, not blindness.

Be assured, also, that the analysis of warrants, as presented on these pages, does not require knowledge of advanced mathematics and its associated language. Basic arithmetic, good judgment, and a willingness to learn are the only prerequisites to mastering the field of warrants. Very often there are rigorous mathematical proofs and theories supporting the tenets of this book. These are appropriately footnoted for those who are interested in further research. However, you may obtain a clear understanding of the field through the study of basic concepts.

Warrants are the most volatile and hence the most dramatic of all securities. When it comes to "could have been" stories, warrants top all others. In 1942 Tri-Continental warrants sold for three cents. Since then they have sold as high as $70. An investment of $300 in 1942 would have been worth $700,000 a quarter of a century later. Another trust warrant, Investment Company of America, experienced a spectacular rise in a much shorter period of time, going from $1.50 to almost $70 in 15 years, 1954 to 1969. This flair for action also works in the other direction. Many warrants have descended from previous peaks, never to rise again. It is usually the lure of another Tri-Continental that attracts the plunger into the warrant market. The skilled investor makes a careful evaluation of the common, considers the risks inherent in the associated warrant, then makes an investment decision. Notice the use of the word "investment" to refer to the decision to purchase a warrant. Warrants are a speculation to the uninformed, an investment to the knowledgeable. Remember the golden rule of warrant investing: Don't buy the warrant unless you would buy the common, don't buy either one unless you have performed a fundamental and favorable analysis of the underlying corporate entity.

I would like to express my appreciation to Daniel Turov, Walter Caroll, and Conrad W. Thomas for their suggestions, which were very helpful in preparing the final draft of this book.

February 1973   S. Lawrence Prendergast

Contents

1. NATURE OF WARRANTS   **1**

Call on Common Stock. Specified Price. Specified Time. Changes in Terms: Price and Time. Dilution. Warrant Agreement. Warrant Certificate. A Limited Security. Traded. Distinguished from Other Convertibles.

2. CREATION OF WARRANTS   **22**

Original Financing. Acquisitions. Mergers. Reorganizations. Other Uses of Warrants. Reasons for Use. Historical Use of Warrants. Future Uses.

3. LEVERAGE AND SOME OTHER RELEVANT CONCEPTS   **54**

Leverage. Intrinsic Value. Premium. Volatility. Adjusted Warrant.

4. PRICE DETERMINATION   **71**

Optioned Stock Price. Expectations for Optioned Stock. Length of Call. Dividends. Listing of Warrant. Usable Senior Securities. Volatility. Existence of Other Convertibles. Steps in Exercise Price. Constraints on Warrant. Call on Other than Common. Dilution Protection. Exchangeable Warrants. Number of Shares Called. Supply and Demand. Unimportant Factors. Price Limits. Norm Price.

5.   THE PURCHASE DECISION   98
     Research Vehicles. What to Consider. When to Buy. When to Sell.
     Buying New Issues. Buy-Sell Guidelines.

6.   SOME PROFITABLE TRADING TECHNIQUES FOR
     WARRANTS   123
     Short Selling. Borrowing for Short Sales. Short Selling as a Trading
     Tactic. The Warrant Hedge. Warrant Hedge Investment. Identifying
     Warrant Hedge Opportunities. Selecting the Hedge Ratio. When to
     Close a Warrant Hedge.

7.   EXPIRING WARRANTS—FORTUNES TO BE MADE   149
     The Short Side. Reversing the Risk. Unbalanced Reverse Hedge.
     Identifying Reverse Hedge Candidates. Choosing the Mix. Using
     Margin to Increase Profits. Trading Canadian Warrants. When to
     Act. Potential Pitfalls. Warrants on the Long Side. The Case for
     Reverse Hedges. What Is Fortune? Attainable Fortunes.

     APPENDIX   188

     BIBLIOGRAPHY   207

     INDEX   211

1

Nature of Warrants

A WARRANT is a negotiable security and as such is a part of the capitalization of the issuing company. In general, the warrant is traded and hence can be acquired in the same manner as other market instruments are acquired; that is, through a registered broker-dealer or from the issuer itself.

The warrant generally entitles the holder to purchase the stock of the issuer subject to limitations on the number of shares purchased, the price paid, and the period of time wherein the warrant is valid. Thus the warrant represents an option on the unissued or treasury stock of the corporation.

CALL ON COMMON STOCK

Warrants are usually options on the common stock of the issuer. Occasionally a warrant represents an option on another type of equity such as preferred stock. Since most outstanding warrants are a call on the common stock of the issuer, they will be discussed as such. This feature enables the owner to "call on" the issuer, requesting that his warrants be converted into the appropriate number of shares of common stock. In this respect warrants are similar to an option on land or any other tangible asset. If one were to buy an option on a piece of property, he could then, during the length of the option, call upon the owner to deliver the property under the terms of the contract. In the same way a warrant is a contractual agreement between the issuer and the holder, enabling the holder to call upon the issuer to deliver stock, which in turn represents the assets and earning power of the issuer. So the warrant represents a call on corporate assets and the title to those assets is in the form of a common stock certificate.

In its simplest form a warrant is the option to buy one share of common stock. However, corporate financial activity after the issuance of a warrant often necessitates a change in the warrant terms, including the number of shares which the holder is entitled to call. As an example, the well-known Tri-Continental Corporation warrants currently entitle the owner to call on 3.13 shares of common. When originally issued these warrants represented a call on one share of common. Subsequent financing in conjunction with the warrant's antidilution features has resulted in the current call terms. Periodic distributions by Tri-Continental keep changing these terms, so it undoubtedly now calls more than the number cited above.

Occasionally a warrant is not a call on the issuer's common, but on that of another firm. This unusual situation can result from mergers and other forms of reorganization. As an example, in 1969 the Cities Service Company issued warrants which were a call on the common stock of Atlantic Richfield

Company. This allowed Cities Service to attempt to liquidate over the life of the warrant a substantial inventory of Atlantic Richfield common which had been held as an investment.

Another classic example of how the shares called feature can become quite interesting is the Hilton Hotel warrants. These warrants, without intervening developments, entitled the owner to call one share of Hilton common at $50 until October 15, 1971. However, in 1964 Hilton International was spun off from the parent, and in 1967 Hilton International was merged into Trans World Airlines. Under the warrant contract's antidilution provisions the warrantholder, as a result of these and other minor financial actions, was entitled to two shares of Hilton Hotels, 0.144375 shares of TWA common and 0.2625 shares of TWA $2.00 convertible preferred stock. As is evident from the above and as is discussed fully in the chapter on price determination, the potential warrantholder should determine exactly what he is purchasing in terms of a call on the assets of one or more firms.

SPECIFIED PRICE

The warrant represents a call on a determinable number of shares of stock at a particular price. This specified price per share is called the *exercise price*. As an example, the Atlas Corporation warrant represents the right to purchase one share of that firm's common at $6.25. The holder of one warrant, wishing to exercise his option, would surrender to the Atlas Corporation the warrant certificate and $6.25 in cash. The issuer, usually through its transfer agent (generally a bank), would then issue a common stock certificate to the former warrantholder. At this point the warrant is retired by the issuer.

At all times the warrantholder must surrender the warrant

certificate to obtain common stock. Occasionally the exercise price is payable in something other than cash. Many warrants are issued in conjunction with other financial instruments, such as interest-bearing bonds. These debt instruments may then be usable at face value in lieu of cash for warrant conversion purposes. If the bond is selling at below *face value* (face is usually $1,000), then it becomes advantageous to use the bonds rather than cash in exercising warrants. As a result of the existence of senior securities, which sell below and are usable at face, an *adjusted exercise price* is computed. Consider a firm that has issued a warrant exercisable at $10.00 per share, one warrant calling one share. Associated with this warrant issue is a bond usable at face ($1,000) in lieu of cash. This bond sells at $700, which is quoted in the papers as "ask 70." Now the warrantholder can go into the bond market, purchase a bond for $700, and surrender it and his 100 warrants for 100 shares of common stock. His adjusted exercise price is 70 percent of $10.00 or $7.00 per share. The total price is $7.00 per share plus whatever the warrant is worth (excluding commissions). Before investing in warrants you should discover what senior securities (bonds or preferred stock) may be usable for exercise purposes.

An adjusted per share exercise price may also result from stock splits and dividends. Assume that XYZ Corporation's warrant entitles the holder to purchase one share of common at $12.50. The company declares a 4 percent stock dividend. Assuming that the warrants are protected against dilution, the warrant now represents a call on 1.04 shares of common at a total cost of $12.50. The adjusted per share exercise price is $12.50 divided by 1.04, or $12.02. In general the adjusted per share exercise price is the cash outlay required to purchase one share of common, assuming prior possession and surrender of the warrant or warrants. This concept is further explored in the later discussion of dilution.

When exercising warrants the holder may find that he is entitled to fractional shares of stock. This arises when the warrant is a call on something other than a round number of shares and the warrantholder does not have a sufficient number of warrants to cover the decimal places in the shares per warrant figure. As an example, the Chris-Craft Industries warrants, currently a call on 1.0534 shares of common, would have to be surrendered in a lot of 10,000 warrants to receive 10,534 shares of common. Converting anything other than a multiple of 10,000 warrants results in fractional shares. In other issues, decimal places are often taken to the fifth position, implying that 100,000 warrants would be required to exercise for nonfractional shares of common. The Chris-Craft warrant agreement stipulates that a cash adjustment will be made for those fractional shares that may otherwise have been lost through exercise. As a rule, stock is not issued in fractional shares. Many mutual funds do so to encourage small monthly investment programs, but most firms do not. The *warrant agreement* stipulates what action should be taken when fractional shares are called. Occasionally the warrantholder is the loser and with a high priced stock this could be significant.

SPECIFIED TIME

In addition to having a specified exercise price, warrants also have a defined life. This period may be limited, or in the case of *perpetual warrants,* be bounded only by the life of the issuer or the complete exercise of all warrants. Most warrants being issued today have a life of one to twenty years, with five being a norm. Companies are reluctant to grant a longer term call which may result in having to sell stock many years hence at a price far below market value. A warrant is exercisable up to and including its *expiration date*. At the close of business on that day it becomes worthless. At least one current warrant has an expiration time of 12:00 noon instead of the customary 5:00 P.M. To avoid such unfortunate stipulations, it is advisable to read the warrant agreement or to exercise prior to the last day of the warrant life. Warrants should never be held through expiration; they should be exercised or sold for what the market will bring. Since the sale price will always cover brokerage fees, a warrant should never be held through expiration.

CHANGES IN TERMS: PRICE AND TIME

During the life of a warrant there may be a change in its terms, specifically to the number of shares called, the exercise price or the length of time during which the option is valid.

Changes in the exercise price are often built into the warrant upon issue. Such changes are usually upward and are called *step-ups*. Thus a warrant with an initial exercise price of $10.00 per share may, through its *escalation clause*, subsequently become a call at $10.50, $11.00, and $11.50 before expiration. The date and amount of *escalation* are stated in the warrant agreement which is drawn up by the issuer. Such a change may be considered explicit in that it is predictable and fully expected by the financial community.

A warrant may also have an optional *step-down* built into its terms. Such clauses usually are worded in such a way that the issuer, at its option, may reduce the exercise price to a specified level for a given period of time. As an example, the issuer may reserve the right to reduce the exercise price by as much as one third for a 30-day period, at the end of which the warrant repossesses its fixed terms. Such step-down clauses are intended to allow the issuer to force exercise, thus eliminating the warrant from the capital structure. However, it should be evident that the activation of such a clause could cause havoc with the market for the warrant and, because of this, the inclusion of such clauses in the warrant agreement is under heavy attack from many quarters. The Board of the American Stock Exchange declared in 1970 that it would refuse to list warrants that contained such step-down or "flush-out" clauses, unless the issuer agrees not to exercise the flush-out option while the warrants are listed. In addition, the issuer must inform the warrantholder of this clause.

Another form of step-down can be effected if the issuer declares debt securities to be usable at face in lieu of cash when exercising, and those debt securities sell below face. Clearly, if a bond selling at 50 percent of face is suddenly declared usable at face, this has the effect of halving the exercise price. Some warrants have preset dates when debt securities become usable or are no longer usable for exercise purposes. However, a few issuers have surreptitiously declared debt temporarily usable to effect a flush-out.

Other changes to the terms of the warrant cannot be foreseen. The issuer, in the waning days of the warrant, may decide to extend its life, much to the chagrin of those who have sold short. The issuer may offer to exchange the existing warrant for a new one having a life greater than that of the old. Such offers of exchange are usually made with a step-up in exercise price as the tradeoff for an extended option on the common. It is interesting to observe how investors evaluate the time and exercise price change. In 1966 McCrory Corporation offered an exchange of warrants resulting in an additional five-year call on its common.

The old warrant was issued in 1961 when McCrory exchanged $40.00 worth of a 5½ percent debenture plus a warrant for each share of Lerner Stores held. This warrant currently represents a call on one share of McCrory common at $20.00 until March 15, 1976. The "new" warrant was created in April of 1966 when McCrory, in taking over Kleins Department Stores, exchanged for Kleins' securities a 5 percent junior, subordinated debenture, due in 1981, plus the

FIGURE 1–1
McCrory Warrant Prices

Date	Old Warrant			New Warrant		
	Hi	*Lo*	*Close*	*Hi*	*Lo*	*Close*
5/11/66	4⅜	4¼	4¼	4⅜	4⅛	4¼
5/12/66	4⅜	4—	4⅛	4⅜	4—	4⅛
5/13/66	4¼	4—	4⅛	4⅛	3⅞	4⅛
6/24/66	3⅞	3¾	3⅞	3⅞	3¾	3⅞

"new" warrant which currently represents a call on McCrory common at $20.00 until March 15, 1976 and at $22.50 to March 15, 1981. Hoping to eliminate the "old" warrant, McCrory, at the time of the Klein acquisition, offered to exchange "new" warrants for "old" warrants. It seemed reasonable to expect warrantholders to surrender the old for the new, obtaining an extra five-year call at a slightly higher exercise price. And yet many investors chose to hold the old warrants and so the firm currently has two warrants outstanding. What is even more amazing, as Figure 1–1 illustrates, is that the two warrants traded within fractions of each other when the new warrant began trading. It is also interesting that recently the two warrants have traded at about the same price on the American Exchange.

Occasionally a warrant is *callable* for redemption by the

firm prior to its expiration date. This is a two-way option in that the issuer, at its discretion, with a minimum notice period of grace can terminate the option agreement. A small redemption fee may be paid to the warrantholder. As an example, the Cayman warrants, issued to expire in 1975, may be called by the company at 50 cents each any time prior to expiration. Such warrants are few and should not be bought unless carefully evaluated. Even the professional warrant trader may be forced to exercise a called warrant, often requiring huge amounts of capital. Possibly a definition of a *professional* and a *nonprofessional* as these terms relate to the market is needed. A professional is one who makes a living by trading in the financial markets of the world. He is capable of absorbing substantial losses in one segment of his portfolio without suffering overall, either financially or emotionally. The nonprofessional is the antithesis of the professional except that he too trades in the financial markets. He should be cognizant of his inability to accept the heavy losses which may occur in substantial risk-reward situations. Most callable warrants represent such a situation.

A warrant usually expires with no residual value. That is, it becomes a worthless piece of paper. The intricacy of the terms of the warrant, as should be evident from the previous discussion, is limited only by the imagination of the issuer. The Commonwealth Edison warrants are exchangeable perpetually at no cost to the holder, for one third share of common. This is an unusual feature and it places a floor on the price of the warrant at one third that of the common.

DILUTION

A warrant may suffer *dilution* when the issuer declares stock dividends, stock splits, or otherwise distributes common stock at a price below the exercise price of the warrant. If a company declares a 100 percent stock dividend and no other significant events occur, the value of its common should be halved. The same effect will result from a two-for-one stock split. The assets and the earning power of the issuer have not changed, and yet there are twice as many shares outstanding. Hence the market will tend to mark down the price of the common by 50 percent. Stockholders also suffer dilution when executive options or convertible securities are exercised. Warrants themselves are a potential dilution to the price of the common.

The warrantholder is most concerned about what provisions have been made to protect him against dilution. The declaration of stock dividends, all other things being equal, depresses the price of the common. Without proper protection against dilution the warrantholder suffers a real loss because his exercise price looks less favorable than it did prior to the dividend. Suppose that a warrant represents the right to purchase one share of common at $10.00 per share. The common currently sells for $10.00. Upon a 100 percent stock dividend the common more than likely would sell down to $5.00. This leaves the warrantholder at a $5.00 disadvantage in his exercise price. In order for the warrantholder to maintain an equivalent option on the common, the issuer would declare that each warrant is now a call on two shares of common at $5.00 per share. Thus the exercise price per share is halved and the number of shares called is doubled. Alternatively, the issuer might also distribute warrants, one for each one currently held, and reduce the exercise price on the old ones to $5.00 to correspond to the new. The mathematics of any other type of split is the same. As an example, Figure 1–2 illustrates the effect of a three-for-two stock split declared by Levin-Townsend (now Rockwood Computer) in 1968. In so doing the issuer provided the warrantholder protection against this form of dilution.

Most warrants issued and currently outstanding are re-garded as *fully protected*. This is a misnomer. It would be more appropriate to say that most warrants are substantially protected. That is, they are most likely fully protected in the event of stock dividends or splits (up or down). They may not

FIGURE 1–2

Notice to holders of

Levin-Townsend Computer Corporation
Warrants, expiring January 15, 1979,
to purchase Common Stock

The Stockholders of the Corporation have approved a three-for-two split of the outstanding shares of Common Stock, payable to stockholders of record on June 28, 1968. As a result of the split, the exercise price per share of the above Warrants has been reduced from $75 to $50 and the number of shares of Common Stock of the Corporation issuable on exercise of the Warrants has been increased from 160,000 shares to 240,000 shares, effective at the close of business on July 18, 1968.

Levin-Townsend Computer Corporation
Howard S. Levin, *President*

Source: *The Wall Street Journal*, May 1968.

be protected against dilution resulting from the exercise of other convertible securities or executive options. Many are not so protected. However, the extent of possible dilution due to such exercise is usually insignificant and as such presents little or no threat to the warrantholder. The amount and type of dilution protection is easily ascertainable and is available from your broker or the issuer.

Warrants may be protected from dilution either in the area

of exercise price, number of shares called, or both. If, upon a 5 percent stock dividend the per share exercise price is reduced 5 percent but the number of shares called is not increased, then the warrant is protected for price only. There would be an upward adjustment in number but no downward adjustment in price if the number of shares called was the only component protected.

WARRANT AGREEMENT

All U.S. companies that wish to issue a significant amount of securities to a wide market must register such an issue with the Securities and Exchange Commission (SEC). Virtually all warrants now coming to market are associated with a firm or another issue large enough to require registration with the SEC. It is the *warrant agreement* that institutions and individuals obtain to ascertain the terms of the warrant. This document is usually available from the SEC in Washington at a nominal copying and mailing fee. The agreement "may" be filed with the SEC as an exhibit with the registration papers covering the issue. This "may" will soon be "must," as the SEC is moving to make the filing of the warrant agreement a mandatory act. Such agreements are often available through the *warrant agent;* that is, the institution or firm that has agreed to act as an advisor to and transfer agent for the issuer.

The warrant agreement is usually quite lengthy and very legalistic in its wording. However, those sections that are most pertinent, such as exercise terms and dilution provisions, are easily identified and, after practice, fairly easily interpreted. Changes to the terms of a warrant are often necessitated by corporate action such as stock splits and dividends. When such an event takes place, the issuer files a certificate with the warrant agent, notifies the securities exchanges on which the warrant trades, and notifies the public that the terms have been adjusted. Notification of the public is usually effected through *authorized newspapers*. Such publications are identified in the warrant agreement. For practical purposes *The Wall Street Journal* and *The New York Times* are good sources for notices of change (see Figure 1–2). However, the notification of a change in warrant terms should come as a confirmation rather than a revelation to the warrantholder. Most corporate actions that affect warrant terms, including mergers and other reorganizations, are fully anticipated by the marketplace.

WARRANT CERTIFICATE

The warrant certificate is not unlike a common stock certificate in appearance. It represents ownership and summarizes the warrant agreement. It is signed by an officer of the issuing firm and may be countersigned by the warrant agent. Figure 1–3 depicts a typical warrant certificate. Most investors never see the actual certificate as it is held by the broker.

A LIMITED SECURITY

Up to this point the positive attributes of a warrant have been enumerated; however, there are certain limitations that distinguish warrants from other instruments such as common stocks and bonds.

Since the warrantholder is not a shareholder, he does not enjoy the privileges of ownership. Hence, he has no voting rights and as such, no matter how large a position he may have in the firm's warrants, is unable to influence operating management or the board of directors. On the other hand,

FIGURE 1-3

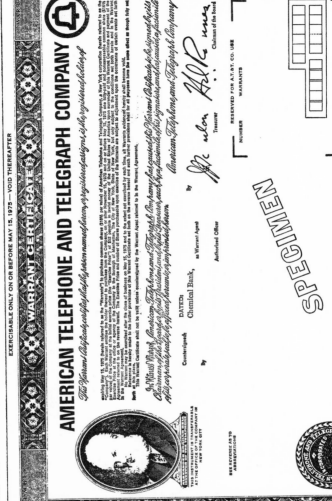

substantial stockholders often are able to influence corporate policy and direction.

Warrantholders do not share in the profits of the firm. This is most evident in the case of dividend payments. Should the dividend be in the form of stock, the warrantholder may be protected against dilution, but he does not receive payment of any kind. Bondholders receive interest payments in consideration of the loan which they have made to the firm. Warrants do not represent a loan and cannot enjoy interest.

As is evident, the warrant in no way represents current ownership in the corporation. Nor does it represent a debt of the corporation. Therefore, the warrantholder does not enjoy a claim on corporate assets in the case of liquidation. The warrant is merely a privilege granted by the issuer to buy common stock at a given price within a stated period of time.

TRADED

Warrants are securities and as such trade very much like common stocks. Due to their unique nature, however, there are certain considerations that the prospective owner of warrants should understand. Warrants may be issued attached (*cum*) to a *senior security*, such as preferred stock or bonds. In this case the issuer specifies whether the warrants are detachable, and if so, when. In most cases the warrants are detachable within a few weeks of the issuance of the *package* or *unit*, which usually consists of a bond and one or more warrants. The announcement of the issuance of the unit may be found in leading newspapers on the day when trading begins. At this point the units are usually traded *over-the-counter* (OTC). The issuer may ultimately list the bond, the warrant, or both. However, it usually takes a few weeks after issuance to gain a listing on one of the stock exchanges. Many bonds and warrants are never listed, always trading OTC. Once trading begins OTC, the National Quotation Bureau follows the price history and publishes a daily listing of all OTC activity, commonly called the *pink sheets*. These price quotations are available on a regional basis, and as such are not always pink or complete with respect to the totality of all issues. However, most brokerage houses and large financial institutions subscribe to the complete service which includes all regional sections as well as a bond supplement. The Eastern Section, which is pink in color, is the largest due to the heavy concentration of market makers in New York. It is from these market makers that the National Quotation Bureau obtains its bid and asked prices. Assuming that a unit is issued, the National Quotation Bureau may show a number of quotes that are indicative of the warrant. First, the bond may trade separately, that is, without the warrant. In this case the bond description includes *XW* or *ex.* Second, the unit may still trade as a unit, in which case the bond description includes *WW* or *cum.* Third, the warrant may trade as *WD*, that is, when detached. In this case delivery of the security cannot possibly take place until the warrant is detachable from the senior security. The date of detachment is specified in the warrant agreement. Fourth, the warrant may be quoted separately. In this case there is no special designation. Finally, a warrant description may be followed by the letters *WI*, indicating that the warrant is trading when, if, and as issued. Should the warrant fail to come to the market, all trades made on a "when" basis are cancelled. Figure 1–4 illustrates how quotes are reported by the National Quotation Bureau. Once in a while a firm will issue warrants that are not detachable, in which case only units would be quoted. This occurs

FIGURE 1–4

National Quotation Bureau "Pink Sheets" (Daily stock price listings for OTC issues)

	SECURITY	MARKET-MAKER	PHONE	BID	ASK
A.	ACETO CHEMICAL CO INC COM	HERZOG & CO INC NY	212 962 0300	7 1/2	8 1/4
		TORPIE & SALTZMAN INC NY	212 425 9619	7 1/2	8 1/4
		MARQUETTE DE BARY CO NY	212 944 4005	7 1/8	
		/MAYER & SCHWEITZER INC NY	212 944 6030	7 1/2	8 1/4
	ACETO CHEM CO INC 73 WTS	/D A DAVIDSON & CO GT FALLS	406 453 1625	4	5
	ACETO CHEM CO INC 76 WTS	/D A DAVIDSON & CO GT FALLS	406 453 1625	2 1/4	3
		HERZOG & CO INC NY	212 962 0300		
		BERNARD L MADOFF NY	212 422 7840	2 1/4	3
		REICH & CO INC NY	212 425 5020	2 1/4	3
B.	ALPHA CAPITAL CORP COM	E L AARON & CO INC NY	212 344 2197	3/4	1 3/8
		/HELFER BRUGHTN&BUKWLTR NY	212 431 6111		
		MAYER & SCHWEITZER INC NY	212 944 6030	5/8	1 1/8
	ALPHA CAPITAL CORP UTS	HELFER BRUGHTN&BUKWLTR NY	212 431 6111		
		E L AARON & CO INC NY	212 344 2197	1	1 1/2
		BIPLANNING SEC FRMNGDLE	212 343 3444		
		MAYER & SCHWEITZER INC NY	212 944 6030	1	1 1/2
	ALPHA CAPITAL CORP 76 WTS	/HELFER BRUGHTN&BUKWLTR NY	212 431 6111	1/4	3/4
		E L AARON & CO INC NY	212 344 2197	1/4	1/2
		MAYER & SCHWEITZER INC NY	212 944 6030	1/4	5/8
C.	AVCO COMUTY DEVEL COM	MANDELBAUM SECS CORP NY	212 248 8753		
		KALB VOORHIS & CO NY	212 425 6000	4 5/8	5 1/8
		SPRAYREGEN SECS INC NY	212 944 4700		
	AVCO COMUTY DEVE 73WTS WI	SPRAYREGEN SECS INC NY	212 944 4700		
	AVCO CORP COM	DISHY EASTON & CO NY	212 425 4130		
		AMSWISS INTL CORP NY	212 425 1067		
		NEW YORK HANSEATIC NY	212 363 4770		
	AVCO CORP WTS WI	H S KIPNIS & CO CG	312 FR21404		
D.	FIRST COLO BKSH INC COM	BOETTCHER & CO NY	212 422 2304	2 7/8	3 3/8
	FIRST COLO BKSH WTS WD	BOSWORTH SULLIVAN DENV	303 892 0827	3	3 1/2
		BOETTCHER & CO NY	212 422 2304	2 7/8	3 3/8
		* G A SAXTON & CO INC NY	212 483 1282		
E.	LIBERTY LOAN 9 1/2-79 WW	/THE CHICAGO CORP CHGO	312 782 4100	102	
	LIBERTY LOAN 9 1/2-79 XW	/THE CHICAGO CORP CHGO	312 782 4100	100	

A—Illustration of common and two different warrants.

B—Illustration of common, units, and warrant.

C—Illustration of warrants trading "when issued."

D—Illustration of warrants trading "when detached."

E—Illustration of bond trading "with warrants" and "without (*X*) warrants."

Source: Pink Sheets, National Quotation Bureau, December 13, 1971.

most often in private placements, where one or more institutions hold the units which are never publicly traded, hence never quoted.

Warrants are usually traded on a *one-to-one* basis. Assume that a firm issues a unit at $1,000, consisting of one bond and twenty warrants. The bond (*XW*) is quoted at 72–75, meaning the *bid* price is $720, the *asked* price is $750. The unit is trading at 111–115, meaning the bid price is $1,110 and the asked price is $1,150, suggesting that the 20 warrants are valued by the market at about $400. The warrant, should it be quoted separately, would approximate 19–20. That is, each warrant is priced on the ask side at $20. The warrant certificate, which is attached to the bond, represents 20 warrants. Hence, should one wish to purchase one warrant, the certificate would have to be split through the transfer agent, assuming that the broker was unable to obtain a previously split certificate. The trading basis is not so easily ascertained where there have been stock splits or dividends. In these cases the protected warrant may trade on a split price basis, or as a call on more than one share at a reduced per share exercise price. The National Association of Securities Dealers (NASD) rules in the case of warrants traded OTC. Trading and the delivery of certificates is conducted based on the day of the corporate action and ruling. You should ask your broker to check the trading basis carefully before placing an order.

Warrants are listed by many major exchanges. The New York Stock Exchange (NYSE) had not listed a warrant for over 20 years, due to the instrument's "speculative nature," until 1970 when A.T.&T.'s warrant was admitted to trading. Since then a number of warrants have been listed on the NYSE. The American (ASE) and most regional and Canadian exchanges list many warrants. A listed warrant enjoys the same benefits of a listing as other financial instruments do. A listed warrant may be bought on margin, assuming that it is not under a restriction imposed by the exchange, the SEC, or your stockbroker. Warrants may also be sold short. This characteristic is not limited to listed warrants, although it is somewhat more difficult to short OTC issues. A complete discussion of short selling appears in Chapter 6.

DISTINGUISHED FROM OTHER CONVERTIBLES

A discussion of the warrant's general characteristics would not be complete without a consideration of its cousins, the other convertible instruments. There are five other standard convertibles: rights, call options, executive options, convertible bonds, and convertible preferred stocks.

Rights may be issued to current stockholders when a firm wishes to float additional common stock. This is a result of the shareholder's *preemptive right,* that is, the right to subscribe to additional shares in proportion to one's current holdings before a sale is made to nonshareholders. A right is very much like a warrant, except that it usually expires a few weeks after issue and is issued to a select group. Rights may be exercised or sold. The exercise price, called the *subscription price,* is usually below the market price for the common, thus creating a value for the rights.

Call options are contracts created by someone other than the issuer of the related security. Calls are generally written by well-to-do individuals who sell them through a *put-and-call broker.* A *contract writer,* in selling a call, agrees to sell the security of a firm at a stated price for a given period of time, usually six months and ten days. The buyer of a call has an instrument very similar to the warrant in its characteristics. Like the stock right, it has a limited life. Like the warrant, it is an option on stock. There are a number of firms specializing in option writing that distribute informative booklets free upon request. Their advertisements are most evident in the *Wall Street Journal* and *The New York Times.*

Executive options are created by the firm for its top executives or critical employees. The option, usually granted upon employment or as an incentive to current employees, represents the right to purchase a stated number of shares at a given price within two specified dates. Presently such option plans must set aside common at the current market price. In most instances a block of shares is set aside by the ownership for the purpose of granting options. Then management allocates such option amounts to individuals as required to attract and retain talent. A typical option might represent a call on 1,000 shares of XYZ Corporation at $40.00 per share, which is today's price, to be valid two years from now for a period of three years. Hence the executive must wait at least two years to exercise in this example.

Convertible bonds are issued by a firm in lieu of straight debt bonds to reduce, relatively, its interest payments and to increase the marketability of the bond. Not only does a bond pay interest, but it is also convertible at face into a fixed number of shares of stock. The convertible feature is very similar to the terms of a warrant, but of course is not detachable or marketable separately. Hence a firm might issue a bond that is convertible into 50 shares of common. Since the bond is usable at *face* (par or $1,000), one could receive 50 shares at $20 each in exchange for the bond. The bond may well trade above or below face, in which case the shares would cost more or less than $20.

Convertible preferred stock is very similar to the convertible bond. The holder, by surrendering the preferred stock and possibly some cash, is entitled to a fixed number of shares of stock. Convertible bonds and convertible preferred stock are usually callable at a certain price. The analysis applied to debt instruments differs somewhat to that for equity so that the convertible bond and preferred stock enjoy distinct markets, from themselves and from other corporate securities.

A very unusual security is the 1969 issue of "C" Preferred by Warner Communications. This issue is unlike a warrant in that it pays a five cent per share dividend. But, like a warrant, it has a couple of conversion privileges, the most important one allowing the holder to surrender the "C" Preferred and $37.00 for one share of common until 1979. This, for all practical purposes, can be considered a dividend-paying warrant. There are a few others like this one, and they are often called "plus cash convertibles," meaning that you must surrender the convertible stock plus some cash to obtain the optioned stock.

2

Creation of Warrants

C ORPORATIONS issue warrants in the same way that they issue other security instruments; that is, the owners must authorize and approve the issue. This may be accomplished at an annual or special meeting of shareholders, or through a proxy solicitation. As a rule, the issuing firm retains the services of an investment banking firm which performs the underwriting. The investment banker acts as a legal advisor, financial advisor, and marketing agent for the issuing firm. Most firms issuing warrants have previously come to market with equity or debt and hence have a working relationship with an investment banker. As a result, that banking house usually acts as the sole or principal underwriter.

Occasionally a firm will issue securities without using an investment banker. Those that resort to such action are either very competent or very foolish. An obvious objective here is the elimination of the underwriter's fee, which can vary from almost nothing to 25 percent or more of the sale value. However, this action is analogous to an individual, untrained in the law, preparing his own will. The results in either case are usually disastrous, the major difference being that the firm usually lives to regret it. Underwriters perform a multitude of services which are beyond the scope of this book; however, none are more significant than the functions of advisor and market maker. Long after an issue hits the market, the underwriting house or group is found supporting and advising the firm. They owe at least this to their own customers who bought the issue.

ORIGINAL FINANCING

Warrants are occasionally issued in conjunction with the original financing of the firm. In this case they are attached to a stock or debt instrument. That is, the warrants are issued in conjunction with another type of security. The combination of warrants and stock or warrants and debt is sold as a unit. Thus a firm may issue one bond with face value of $1,000 and 20 warrants attached for a price of $1,000, or $950, or $1,050. Similarly, one share and one warrant may be sold for $5.00. The components of a unit are never separable on the original sale. If you want to buy the warrant you must also buy the attached security or wait for the secondary market. However, there is nothing to prevent the buyer from selling the unwanted component immediately, even before delivery, or in some cases, even before issuance. To date, no firm has issued warrants and only warrants as its original financing. To do this, it would at the same time have to authorize the shares on which the warrants are a call. Having gone through the trouble of this authorization and registration with the SEC or State Securities Commission, the firm would find it logical to sell some stock at the same time. More importantly, however, it would be almost impossible to sell a warrant which represents a call on a security which has no market price and following.

Warrants are often issued with stock as original financing in order to meet corporate obligations. Promoters and underwriters are frequently compensated for services rendered with warrants. Thus the underwriter may accept cash, stock, warrants, or some combination thereof in consideration for services performed. Promoters, in addition to receiving stock as a rule, may receive warrants for forming the company. They may be allowed to purchase warrants for a nominal price, such as 25 cents each, in addition to receiving them outright as part of their compensation.

ACQUISITIONS

An acquiring company will often issue warrants and other securities to be used in exchange for the assets, liabilities, and capital of the acquired. The acquired's business and securities, that is, its stocks, bonds, and warrants, are assumed by the acquiring firm in exchange for its own package of securities.

Acquisitions are often made through a tender offer to the object firm's ownership. Such a move is more appropriately called a take-over attempt. Such tender offers are sometimes unsolicited and heavily fought by the management of the object company. Figure 2–1 illustrates the nature and complexity of such an offer.

The announcement of a tender offer usually has some dramatic ramifications. The stock price of the object firm will move toward the value of the security or combination of securities that the source firm is offering. Secondly, the at-

FIGURE 2–1

IMPORTANT NOTICE OF EXCHANGE OFFER
TO HOLDERS OF CAPITAL STOCK OF

Radio Engineering Products Limited

FOR ANY AND ALL SHARES TENDERED, BY

Nytronics, Inc.

A registration statement, filed with the Securities and Exchange Commission, became effective on September 9, 1969 covering the issuance of:

846,000 Shares of Capital Stock
(par value $.50 per share)
of Nytronics, Inc.
and
Warrants to Purchase
900,000 Shares of Capital Stock

Nytronics, Inc. offers in exchange for each share of Capital Stock of Radio Engineering Products Limited, 1.41 shares of Capital Stock of Nytronics, Inc. and 1.5 Warrants to Purchase 1.5 shares of Capital Stock of Nytronics, Inc. The Exchange Offer is subject to the terms and conditions specified in the Prospectus and is a revision of the Exchange Offer made by Prospectus dated July 9, 1969. REP shareholders who have tendered their shares of Capital Stock pursuant to the original offer will be automatically entitled to the benefit of this revised Exchange Offer including the right to withdraw the shares previously tendered.

THE EXCHANGE OFFER WILL EXPIRE AT 5 P.M. NEW YORK TIME ON JANUARY 15, 1970, UNLESS EXTENDED, BUT MAY BE TERMINATED BY OCTOBER 15, 1969 BY NYTRONICS, INC. IF NOT ACCEPTED BY 90% OR MORE OF THE SHAREHOLDERS OF RADIO ENGINEERING PRODUCTS LIMITED

Copies of the Prospectus and the Form of Tender relating to the Exchange Offer may be obtained from the Exchange Agent and Forwarding Agent, as well as from the Dealer Managers or from other qualified dealers soliciting acceptances under the terms of the Exchange Offer.

Dealer Managers:

STERLING, GRACE & CO.	GAIRDNER & COMPANY LIMITED
39 Broadway	Box 53, Toronto Dominion Centre
New York, New York 10006	Toronto 111, Canada

Exchange Agent:	*Forwarding Agent:*
THE BANK OF NEW YORK	CANADA PERMANENT TRUST COMPANY
Corporate Agencies Division	Stock Transfer Department
6th Floor, 20 Broad Street	600 Dorchester Blvd. West 1901 Yonge Street
New York, New York 10005	Montreal 101, Quebec Toronto 295, Ontario

Members of the National Association of Security Dealers, Inc. or Investment Dealers Association of Canada or members of the New York, American, Montreal, Toronto or other recognized Stock Exchanges in Canada who have lawfully solicited or obtained the tender of shares will be paid a commission of $.35 per share, provided the name of the dealer appears on such Form of Tender.

This announcement is neither an offer to sell nor a solicitation of an offer to buy or exchange the securities referred to above. The Exchange Offer is made only by the Prospectus, copies of which may be obtained in any state or jurisdiction only from such brokers or dealers as may lawfully offer the securities in such state or jurisdiction.

Source: *The New York Times,* September 17, 1969, p. 65.

tacked firm usually retaliates with heated, open letters to shareholders or, more drastically, with a countermove of its own. A battle of words may be waged in the major financial newspapers for many months before the outcome is known.

Warrants played a major role in one of the most sensational take-over attempts of the 1960s. Leasco Data Processing Equipment Corporation's attempted acquisition of Chemical Bank of New York rocked Wall Street and will continue to have repercussions for years to come. Leasco, then the largest of the computer leasing firms, with assets of $400 million, attempted to acquire Chemical, the sixth largest bank in the United States, with over $9 billion in assets. Whenever the acquiring firm cannot pay for the assets of the object firm solely with stock, even given a large disparity in price-earnings ratios, it must offer something else. This is usually warrants or convertible debentures. Even with the warrants and the large difference in price-earnings ratios, Leasco's offer seemed amazing. Banks, brokerage houses, and politicians ran to Chemical's side, and the day was won, at least temporarily. However, the power of the warrant as a tool in huge acquisition attempts had been demonstrated. Many less dramatic exchanges are made on a regular basis. There is about one warrant per month being issued in conjunction with mergers and acquisitions.

A most unusual acquisition bid was announced in May of 1969. Investors Funding Corporation announced that it would offer only stock purchase warrants in exchange for the outstanding shares of Congressional Life Insurance Company of New York. What is even more astounding is that Congressional Life's management said it would recommend that its shareholders accept this unusual offer. This action tends to discredit those who argue that warrants are "funny money" because they do not represent ownership in a company. Funny they may seem, but at least these two firms were agreed on their value.

MERGERS

A merger results in the creation of a new firm and the extinction of the two that merged into the one. Warrants may arise out of such a combination, as was the case recently when United National Investors was formed from the merger of United Investors Corporation and First National Real Estate Trust. A package of convertible preferred stock, common stock, and warrants was issued.

In the early sixties, Symington-Gould and Wayne Pump merged to form Symington-Wayne. Here warrants were attached to a bond and distributed to the shareholders of the two original firms in exchange for their securities.

REORGANIZATIONS

Warrants often arise in the reorganization and recapitalization of firms. Firms that have had their problems and as a result have a very awkward capital structure in terms of debt-equity ratios, dividend arrears, or other such symptoms may ask shareholders to accept warrants in exchange for some other security. Hence, a bond issue, currently in default and selling somewhere between 20 and 50, may be exchanged for warrants. Bondholders are usually convinced to accept the junior security because a defaulted bond indicates serious problems that may result in nonpayment of principal when the bond is due. The liquidation value to bondholders is usually quite insignificant, 15 cents on the dollar being a

representative number. A classic example of such a reorganization occurred in 1952. Alleghany Corporation, an investment trust whose common shares traded on the New York
Stock Exchange, had 237,000 shares of $100 par Series A
preferred stock outstanding. The preferred had dividends in
arrears amounting to $116.75 per share. With major prob-
lems continuing, it was unlikely that the firm would be able
to pay the almost $28 million needed to put the preferred
back in good stead. In addition, due to the preferred's inden-
ture, no dividends could be paid on the common until the
preferred arrears were paid. A significant percentage of the
preferred was held by common stockholders. To say the least,
the trust had an unhappy ownership. With the preferred
shareholders in a real fix, the company offered to exchange
a new 5 percent bond with 20 warrants attached for each
$100 preferred stock. Each warrant, which was even more
attractive since it was perpetual, was a call on Alleghany
common at $3.75 per share. This offer was extended to the
first 100,000 shares of preferred tendered and was quickly
snapped up. As a result, two million warrants were created
and they now trade on the American Exchange. Those preferred stockholders who tendered their stock made a very
fortunate decision. Within a year the warrant price went from
75 cents to almost $4.00. Thus the exchange had already
resulted in a two-thirds recovery of dividends in arrears.
Since 1953 the warrant has sold as high as $25, being one
of the most discussed and popular warrants available. The
assignment of perpetual life was instrumental in creating a
following for the warrant that enhances its marketability. As
a result of the reorganization, the preferred holders benefited
by having a new sinking fund bond plus 20 warrants, and
the common shareholders benefited due to the improvement
in capital structure. Neither group could have come out so

well, all other factors considered constant, without the warrant instrument.

OTHER USES OF WARRANTS

Warrants are often issued in conjunction with other securities in order to raise working capital for the issuer. Tenneco, Inc., a huge natural gas and oil producer, recently issued 10-year debentures with 2,500,000 warrants attached. In this case the funds generated were used to eliminate some short term notes and to expand working capital. Granite Management Services, one of the larger computer leasing firms, recently sold a unit consisting of one warrant and five shares of common. Many new and emerging companies have issued similar units.

A few firms have issued warrants as dividends. Cash and stock dividends are quite common; warrants are not. In March of 1969 Fuqua Industries announced that it was replacing its 20 cent annual cash dividend payment with a new dividend policy involving both warrants and stock.

Occasionally a warrant is sold to present common shareholders for cash. These sales are made outside of any other financing, such as debt issuance. Such was the case in 1964 when Mid-America Pipeline sold warrants to shareholders and placed a floor on the market price by stipulating that the warrants were exchangeable upon expiration for one-half share of common.

REASONS FOR USE

The most common, if incomplete, reason given for the use of a warrant is that it is a "sweetener." That is, the warrant makes an otherwise undesirable security salable. The contention is that bonds or stocks, which could not be as easily sold otherwise, are given an added kicker through a conversion privilege or a warrant. Usually the exercise price of the warrant is above the current market price of the common, giving the warrant no immediate intrinsic value. At the present time the issue price premium ranges from zero to 25 percent with most major issues coming with an exercise price 10 to 15 percent above the common. The concept of a sweetener has been held over from the thirties and early fifties when some senior issues may have been helped by the attached warrants. Today, however, their use is dictated by corporate planning and pure economics.

In a very obvious way the use of warrants reduces the costs of financing. The issuer, assuming a unit of debt or stock in conjunction with a warrant, obtains a free ride in the prospectus; that is, the firm incurs a minimum additional charge in fees to gain a license to issue stock through warrant exercising over a period of time. This creates a distribution of cash flow rather than a large, initial influx. Of course there is the risk that the price of the common may fall and remain below the exercise price, resulting in limited conversion of warrants and the resultant sale of stock. Assuming that conversion is attractive to the holder, warrants provide the firm with an excellent vehicle for floating its common stock. Only about half of all warrants issued in the last 10 years have been exercised, in spite of a generally "up" market.

The real advantage in the use of warrants comes in the tax savings that can accrue to the issuer. Firms planning to issue convertible bonds or straight debt should carefully consider issuing debentures with warrants attached. A tax benefit arises from the fact that the allowable deduction for amortization of the bond discount takes into consideration the value of the warrant. Assume that a firm wished to issue debt today.

It might issue a 7 percent, 25-year bond, convertible into common stock 15 percent above the current market price. In this case the issuer could deduct for tax purposes the interest expense incurred each year. It is also possible to amortize the issuing expense, but this is usually small relative to the interest expense. Hence, in this example, the firm would have annual expenses of $70 per $1,000 bond with an aftertax cost of $35, assuming a 50 percent tax bracket.

Examine what would have happened if the firm had chosen warrants instead of a convertibility feature. The firm would be able to allocate the proceeds of the unit's sale over both the bond and the warrant. Relying on the Investment Bankers Association of America's study of warrants and options,[1] the firm might establish an initial value of about $320 for the warrant. This means that the firm can allocate $320 to the warrant and $680 to the bond. The $680 assigned to the bond should agree with the value assigned by current bond tables. If it is more or less, the differential should be used to adjust the $320 allocated to the warrant. Hence the firm not only writes off $70 per year for interest expense, but is entitled to amortize the $320 as a bond discount over the 25-year life of the bond, providing another $13 per year in deductions. The after tax cost would be $28.50 versus $35 for a straight debt or convertible bond issue. In addition, there is no tax liability when and if the warrants are exercised. Proceeds from the sale of stock in a warrant conversion are considered paid-in capital, just as if the firm had sold stock. In this particular point there are no differences between the convertible bond and warrants. Should the warrants expire unexercised, the firm does not have to recognize option income as is the general rule for other types of options.

---

[1] Investment Bankers Association of America, unpublished study, October 8, 1963, p. 39.

At this writing the Internal Revenue Service is challenging this point and has brought suit against LTV Corp., issuer of numerous warrants. The tax authorities would like to have companies recognize proceeds derived from the sale of unexercised warrants as ordinary income. If the IRS prevails, it will have a profound effect on new warrant issues. Already, warrant issuers are protecting their interests by including warrant provisions, such as the right to call, extend the life of, or reduce the exercise price of warrants, as expiration nears. In so doing they would force exercise and thus avoid the tax liability. The final decision in this case will probably go in the government's favor.

The advantage of warrants over the convertible bond feature should be quite clear. It is impossible to amortize, in a similar manner, the possible discount due to the conversion feature of a bond. The advantage of the warrant package lies in your being able to ascertain an immediate value for the warrant. This is done by obtaining an investment banker's assessment of the warrant's value and applying for a Treasury ruling. The object of the exercise is to obtain the highest possible value for the warrant (bond discount). There currently are heated discussions in government, finance, and legal circles concerning the tax treatment of the warrant-bond issue, and the investment banker should make a close scrutiny of the current opinion prior to issuance.

In the case of acquisitions, it is important to the shareholders involved that the exchange of stock be tax free in character. Since warrants do not give the holders the same rights of ownership that stock bestows, the IRS has stated that warrants constitute "other property." In order to preserve the tax-free character of an exchange, the strict requirement of "solely voting stock" applies to 80 percent of the exchange, allowing up to 20 percent to be other property, that is, liabilities and warrants. In many cases, however, the assumed liabilities leave little or no space for warrants. Since warrants are nonequity and nonvoting securities, they present some real problems in acquisitions. If the 20 percent rule is insufficient, there may be another remedy. Installment sales[2] are being used in increasing numbers. This method does not maintain the tax-free character, but rather it lightens the tax bite on a sale of securities. A selling stockholder may choose the installment method of reporting gains if his total sale price exceeds $1,000 and if the payments received in the year of the acquisition do not exceed 30 percent of the total sale price. As an example:

An investor who paid $500 for common stock 10 years ago sells it for $1,200, with payment to be received in cash at the rate of $200 a year for six years. Since the price is more than $1,000, and $200 is less than 30 percent of $1,200, election of the installment sale is permissible. One sixth of the capital gain of $700, or $116.67, should be recognized each year as the $200 payment is received.

Clearly, the selling stockholder finds this procedure more attractive than immediately recognizing all $700 of gain for tax purposes, while receiving only $200 in the year of sale.

By contrast, consider this alternative mode of payment, which is not eligible for installment treatment: The selling stockholder receives nonvoting preferred stock for his common through a tender offer. As in the cash settlement, the transaction is completely taxed; but, since he gets more than 30 percent of the purchase price in the year of sale (in fact, he gets 100 percent of the payment), he cannot use the installment method for reporting the gain.[3]

Obviously, the use of this method is most appropriate when the acquired firm is privately held or has a limited number of large shareholders. The real value of the installment sale

---

[2] Samuel L. Hayes III and Henry B. Reiling, "Sophisticated Financing Tool: The Warrant," *Harvard Business Review* (January–February 1969), p. 146 ff.

[3] Hayes and Reiling, "The Warrant," p. 146 ff.

arises out of the fact that the IRS, in determining whether 30 percent of the selling price was received in the first year or not, excludes evidence of indebtedness from the determination. As a result, all debt instruments are excluded.

Warrants, when considered in light of other methods of financing, have some decided advantages. When compared to common stock, warrants present some interesting benefits to the issuer. They do not command a dividend, as stock often does, and as such are not a consideration in the cash flow budgeting problems. Since warrants will never pay a dividend, the marketplace is capital gains oriented rather than payout inclined. There are no outside pressures to initiate, increase, or not pass a dividend. Such pressures are felt at one time or another by most corporations. Warrants may be issued and capital raised without immediately increasing the common stock "float" and without immediately creating a whole new group of voting stockholders. Closely held firms, wishing to remain the same, find that warrants provide good protection against the creation of another large blockholding with its directorship and control implications. Warrants, once detached from a senior security, tend to trade in "small" rather than "large" hands. Where an institution is likely to take down 100,000 shares of stock in a given firm for $3 million, it is unlikely to take down 100,000 warrants for $1 million. There are many reasons for this phenomenon. The acceptability and marketability of warrants are still questioned by many. Warrants fluctuate in price more than the corresponding stock will, causing wide and sometimes disturbing changes in asset values, often at the end of a period when investors will be viewing the managed fund's portfolio. Many institutions and fund managers are prevented from purchasing warrants because of the fund's charter which may have been written many years back. It has taken pension fund trustees 30 years to realize that there are instruments other than bonds that are appropriate to fund portfolios and long-term capital growth. The acceptance period for warrants has at least a 10-year lag behind that for common stock. This acceptance, when gained, will be only partial; that is, warrants will have marketability and respectability due to the nature of the issuer. Warrants will never provide ownership in a corporation, however, and this is something that is valued in our financial and human system.

When compared to straight debt, warrants provide some advantages to the issuer. There is no interest to be paid and hence no debt coverage ratios to worry about. Should additional financing be required, $10 million outstanding in warrants is much more readily accepted by an underwriter who is worried about capital structure than an equivalent amount of debt or common is. Warrants enjoy a state of limbo with all but the accountants, who justifiably require full dilution earnings reports. Since warrants do not represent ownership, they are, for corporate planning purposes, only a call on the stock. One of the most interesting benefits of warrants over straight debt is that the debt must be paid back at some point, but warrants may never be. A firm issuing debt must repay or refinance. The U.S. government is just about the only domestic organization that is able to roll over its debt continuously and with impunity. Corporations end up paying off sooner or later. If a warrant is issued with an exercise price of 115 percent of the common with step-ups of 10 percent per year for its life, there is a fair chance that the common price will never exceed the exercise price by enough of a margin to make converting profitable. In this case the warrant will expire and the firm will realize a full profit on the original sale price! There has been no dilution of equity and the firm has permanent use of the funds received for the warrants. The benefit may also be an indirect one, such as a lower interest coupon on a bond with warrants attached than would have been required without them. Another factor that works in the issuer's favor is that warrants are bought to be sold, not exercised. Warrantholders do not start thinking about exercise until the expiration date is near. So even if the common goes considerably above the exercise price, warrants will tend to be held rather than exercised until pre-expiration trading begins, which is about 18 months before the expiration date. As a rule, if the common price goes below the exercise price in the warrant's waning days, the instrument will be held. There is always a certain percentage of conversion, but never 100 percent so long as there is no profit to be obtained. *Arbitrageurs* do an excellent job of maintaining price parity between the common and the warrant. If there is a distortion in price it is on the warrant side with the warrant's premium making its exercise unprofitable.

As should be evident there are many significant reasons why corporations use warrants. Unfortunately, there are a number of corporate officers who do not even consider this instrument in corporate planning. This phenomenon is due to fear or a lack of understanding. It is interesting to note the large number of newer companies, run by younger men, now issuing warrants. Some will say this is the "sweetener" angle rather than sophisticated financing; however, the latter should prove to be the case. There also are many large, "Fortune 500" type firms now issuing warrants. These firms are generally those with the most capable finance men.

HISTORICAL USE OF WARRANTS

During the 1920s and 1930s warrants enjoyed the best and the worst of popularity. The last phase, being the worst, is unfortunately the one best remembered. As a result, there is the popular notion that warrants are issued by floundering firms. Unfortunately, many of the trusts and holding companies that were created in the 1920s issued warrants. These same firms fell the fastest and hardest when the bubble burst. One of the best examples is the case of warrants issued by American & Foreign Power Company which were attached to preferred stock. At their top price of $175 during 1929 these warrants had a market value of over $1 billion. In 1952 the firm was recapitalized and the warrants were dropped, having no value whatsoever.

The first known warrant is that of American Power & Light, issued in 1911. During the 1920s, warrants grew in popularity and were often exploited by the issuer. Warrants suffered a decline in the 1930s that resulted in only a handful of actively traded warrants being outstanding in 1950. Since then the number has grown so that there are now over 300 actively traded U.S. warrants and about one hundred Canadian issues. Warrants are now issued by solid, large firms. These include A.T.&T., Avco, Braniff Airlines, Commonwealth Edison, Leasco Data, United Utilities, Zayre, and many more. In addition, we have seen registrations by many other reputable firms, indicating a continuation of this trend.

Warrants are being issued in great numbers by new and emerging firms. Many have been issued by the equipment leasing firms. This is due in part to the great portion debt plays in their capital structures. It is also true that these firms, due to the very nature of their business, retain highly sophisticated finance men who recommend the use of warrants.

Private placements account for a large segment of warrant issuance, one which is generally considered to be greater than the volume of public distribution. Many institutions, especially investment bankers and insurance companies, have

FIGURE 2–2
Private Placement Notice with Warrants

These Notes have not been and are not being offered to the public.
This advertisement appears only as a matter of record.

NEW ISSUE
December 14, 1971

$30,000,000

Harnischfeger Corporation

Notes due 1991

With Warrants

Direct placement of the above Notes was negotiated ·
by the undersigned.

The First Boston Corporation.

Investment
Securities

NEW YORK   BOSTON   CHICAGO   CLEVELAND   LONDON
LOS ANGELES   PHILADELPHIA   PITTSBURGH   SAN FRANCISCO   ZURICH

Source: *The New York Times*, December 14, 1971, p. 71.

been taking warrants in consideration for loans or underwriting activities. Read almost any prospectus on a new issue for a small firm and you will find the underwriter receiving a warrant as part of his selling commission or in consideration for legal and other advice. Figure 2–2 illustrates how the public is often notified of such a placement. Unfortunately, due to the warrant agreement, the privately placed warrants are almost never publicly traded.

As has been shown, the public acceptance of warrant issues has grown tremendously within the last 20 years. Such acceptance is best illustrated by the positions that professionally managed money has taken in these instruments. A sample of annual reports shows the use of warrants is on the upswing in the portfolios managed by the professionals.

Warrants are also enjoying far greater marketability as they are being listed in greater numbers by almost all major exchanges. The American Stock Exchange (ASE) lists over 70 warrants which account for about 10 percent of the total trading volume on the exchange, even though the number of warrants as a percentage of ASE-listed securities is only about 6 percent. In addition, in 1969 the ASE revised[4] its listing requirements for warrants. The common or other "underlying" securities must be listed on the ASE or the New York Stock Exchange, there must be a minimum public distribution of at least 500,000 warrants, and the issuer must agree to split warrants in the same ratio as stock. These requirements are in addition to the tangible-asset test and other standard tests that the issuer must pass for any type of ASE listing. In 1970 the A.T.&T. warrant was the first warrant in many years to be listed on the New York Stock Exchange. It has been followed by a score of others at this writing, and the number mounts.

The OTC market accounts for most warrant issues. This market is enjoying higher volume and better communications, and thus provides better marketability for warrants. Warrants are being issued in larger numbers by a given issuer, creating the potential of a stable market. The average number of warrants outstanding per issuer is steadily advancing. This trend should continue as larger and more soundly

---

[4] *American Investor*, September 1969, p. 14.

financed firms utilize the warrant. The OTC market will be fully automated in the not too distant future. This action will, among other important things, raise the "visibility" and marketability of warrants, even including the so-called "thin" issues.

Warrant-bond units are enjoying increased marketability. Individual investors, when weighing a unit and straight debt issue, are naturally drawn to the warrant unit by the ever increasing interest rates which result in lower bond prices. They feel that the attached warrants provide some protection against inflation. A generous bond coupon previously provided a "floor" for straight debt issues; however, over the last 15 years those investors long on bonds have experienced a sinking foundation. To roll over their bonds for higher coupons is to take a long-term loss on older debt issues. Although there is no guarantee that interest rates, and consequently bond yields, will continue to rise, investors develop a mental set which becomes cast in cement over time. The disenchantment with straight debt will end when bond prices rise and interest rates fall significantly. Although they have receded from 1970 highs, interest rates are still relatively high. The lowering of rates is inevitable and should not be too long in coming. In the meantime the public will favor debt with a convertible feature.

Institutional investors have also generated a healthy demand for warrant-bond units. In many cases the charters of such institutions as life insurance companies and pension funds prevent them from holding equity, but allow debt and preferred stock. Convertible bonds and warrant-bond units become attractive to such institutions. Institutional investors account for almost all private placements involving a warrant-bond package.

Individual investors are often attracted to the warrant-bond unit by the significant difference in margin requirements between equity and debt. This phenomenon is less pronounced in times of the high prime rates currently being experienced. However, in the late fifties and early sixties it was possible to cover the interest paid for margin buying with the coupon on the bonds purchased. Banks have historically loaned 80 percent or more on high-grade convertibles and bond-warrant units. Therefore an investor may be able to put up 20 cents to get $1.00 working for him while the coupon on the bond covers the interest on the 80 cents borrowed. His leverage is further enhanced by the warrant or convertible feature. Professionals dealing in U.S. government issues have often obtained 95 percent financing, looking for a minor drop in interest rates to create a highly leveraged capital advance. Such operations require huge amounts of capital which the average investor does not have, hence the individual is attracted to the more widely fluctuating convertibles.

Perpetual warrants enjoyed good marketability a number of years ago, the most notable issues being the still existent issues of Atlas Corporation, Alleghany Corporation, Investment Company of America, and Tri-Continental Corporation. For a number of years firms shied away from granting indefinite term calls on their common. Recently, perpetuals have again been marketed, highly successfully. Canadian Gas & Energy Fund Ltd., Stokely-Van Camp, Inc., and Texas International Airlines, Inc. have issued perpetual warrants. From a balance sheet standpoint this appears to be a desirable thing to do since perpetuals do not require a line in the capitalization section. Instead, their existence is found in a footnote. Although this footnote treatment is due to change as more standard and forthright accounting practices come into use, the perpetual warrant should continue to be a highly marketable instrument. Both the issuer and holder find them attractive. In spite of the reluctance to grant a "forever" call on stock at a fixed price, the use of perpetual warrants should increase in the next few years.

As is evident from Figure 2–3 the volume of public and private debt issues making use of the convertible or warrant feature has grown dramatically during the 1960s.

Such growth is in no small part due to the increasing acceptance and marketability of such units. The convertible bond and preferred stock issues have led the way. In so doing

FIGURE 2–3
Growth in Issuance of Warrants

Year	Bonds with Warrants		Stock with Warrants	
	Number	Amount*	Number	Amount*
1967	26	$304	11	$ 12
1968	30	380	35	233
1969	38	657	85	645
1970	39	721	67	796

* Dollar figures in millions.
Source: *Investment Dealer's Digest.*

they have enhanced the status of the warrant. As the issuer and consumer become more sophisticated we can expect at least two things to happen. First, the growth in the use of convertible securities including warrants will continue. Second, the terms of conversion will become more complex and interesting. The increasing use of flush-out clauses and redeemable (callable) warrants reveals this trend. Some recent call provisions make the warrant analysis game a real challenge.

Tight money has given a tremendous boost to the growth of warrant use. Firms, being cash poor, are able to grant a lower coupon rate with the convertible feature. With prime rates ranging between 6 and 9 percent, this becomes a significant consideration. Easy money, should it reappear, might retard the growth of warrant issuance, but the basic job of education and acceptance will have been accomplished. The high interest rates have also given an unusual push to warrants. The 1960s produced the *conglomerate* corporation, a firm with many products and untested ideas. The emergence of these firms was partly due to ingenious entrepreneurs, such as James Ling, partly due to a demand for such a movement on the part of the consumer paying for the stock, but mostly due to the tight money situation. Cash-rich firms found themselves as targets for cash-poor, "paper-rich" companies. Acquiring substantial assets, often including large sums of working capital, for a large supply of new equity or debt seemed like a great idea. Convertible bonds and warrants were often used to build the conglomerate. This was done to such an extent that many Wall Street critics labeled the resultant issues "funny money." In the short run such publicity has damaged the creditability of warrants. Many such firms enjoyed large price-earnings ratios, only to plummet in the market break of 1969. Again, the public viewed the issues as something other than funny. Finally, the accounting fraternity has justifiably taken the conglomerates to task, pushing stock values even lower. However, the storm will blow over and in the long run many of these firms will emerge as major corporations with large asset values as well as earning power. The warrant should benefit in that development.

Besides the use of warrants by conglomerates, other more sedate firms have successfully acquired, been acquired, merged, or in some way altered their capital structure utilizing the warrant. The boom of the sixties placed a heavy burden on firms to generate progressively better earnings reports. Many firms, unable to accomplish this via the accepted retained earnings, research and development, capital investment route, decided to buy their bottom line earnings with stock. In many cases there was a set of complementary products and services that resulted in stronger and more viable entities. The far-flung conglomerates are representative of those that failed, at least temporarily. Those that succeeded have done a great service to the warrant. Government and investment community pressures may retard the growth in the number of mergers, but the use of the warrant has been established.

Closely related to the growth in number of acquisitions and mergers is the recent controversy over reported earnings per share. Until 1969 firms were able to issue convertible securities for bottom line profits and, ipso facto, boost reported earnings. The public loved it and it wasn't until some of the glitter wore off the conglomerates that the public demanded the true story. The Accounting Principles Board of the American Institute of Certified Public Accountants ruled that earnings must be reported on a fully diluted basis, taking into consideration all outstanding "residual" securities. Today firms report their earnings both ways, and the diluted per-share earnings figure appears in the body of the report rather than in a hard-to-find footnote.

The consumer's demand for performance and the earnings-per-share reporting rulings have sent corporate financial officers back to the drawing boards. The result has been a marked decrease in the ratio of equity to debt, both in existence and being issued. The claim on assets has moved more toward debtors, less toward ownership. The name of the game is to squeeze as much debt as possible in the capital structure in order to achieve maximum performance for the equity structure. Such operations are called "trading on the equity." Many accountants frown on the issuance of large amounts of debt that require substantial fixed payments. Unlike the dividend, these payments cannot easily be suspended in rough economic periods. The fact that many major corporations have outstanding debt yielding over 10 percent per annum is proof enough that the public is also apprehensive about the situation. In order to exceed what in the past have been "acceptable" debt-equity ratios for various industries, many firms have used the warrant.

Many issuers and potential issuers of warrants are also intrigued by the control which a debt-warrant unit provides but the convertible bond does not. The flush-out clauses, mentioned previously, allow the issuer to force exercise. This is done when market and cash flow conditions make conversion favorable to the issuer rather than the holder. By stipulating that the warrants be exercised with cash, rather than the senior security usable at face, the issuer is able to control the amount of equity dilution that the issue potentially creates. If the issuer's common is selling for $50 per share upon a convertible bond issuance, then the conversion, assuming no markup on the convertible, results in 20 new shares of stock. That is, the bondholder has the right to surrender his bond at face value for 20 shares of stock. A comparable bond-warrant issue, however, may not require a call on 20 shares of stock. In fact, a sample of convertible bonds and bond-warrant units of issuers in the same industry with comparable financial structures indicates that the firm issuing warrants is able to obtain more dollars for less potential dilution. Hence, the use of bond-warrant units tends to increase the debt capacity of the firm, thus increasing its leverage or ability to get more dollars working per share outstanding on a completely diluted basis. An added attribute of the warrant is that it tends to be held rather than exercised, even through expiration in many cases. Hence, the real and final dilution tends to be less than might be experienced with convertible bonds. Convertible bonds, assuming a favorable common price, tend to be exercised throughout their life on a rather even distribution basis. This is not the case with warrants which tend to be held for trading purposes until close to expiration. This situation in convertible bond distribution is in no small part due to the fact that institutions favor and hold convertibles, exercising in an orderly fashion when conditions are right. If an institution purchases a convertible bond, it has made a tacit decision to purchase the common. Such is not the case with the warrant buyer. The difference in investment psychology favors the issue of warrants.

The use of the conversion feature, whether it be bond or warrant, allows the issuer to borrow more for less current cost than would be incurred with straight debt. The difference between the coupon on the straight debt issue and that on the convertible or bond-warrant issue is often called a sweetener. There is a tradeoff, however, between the lower debt carrying costs and the possible sale of stock below market at a future date upon conversion or exercise. The issuer should evaluate this tradeoff carefully when the exercise price and number of shares called is set. With convertible bonds these are not independent decisions. Assuming a face value of $1,000, the selection of $50 as the exercise price results in 20 shares of potential dilution and the selection of $10 as the exercise price results in a hundred shares of potential dilution. Since the exercise price is usually within 15 percent of the current common market price, the convertible bond provides little leeway in setting the number of shares called. With a bond-warrant issue, however, the number of shares called is easily manipulated. Although the option price cannot be much more than 15 to 20 percent above the current common price, lest the conversion feature be completely discounted, the number of warrants called is a carefully selected figure. Consideration is given to the firm's internal rate of return or cost of capital, potential dilution, and debt-to-equity ratios and carrying cost ratios that the investment community will be looking at. The object in setting the number of shares is to obtain the best possible coupon for the least possible future cost in terms of foregone capital and dilution. The example which follows illustrates some of the considerations given to the areas mentioned by a typical financial officer. The Acme Corporation is considering a $5 million bond-warrant issue with 20 warrants attached to each bond, each warrant exercisable for five years at $55, which is $10 above the current market price for the common. The investment banker feels that he can market such an issue with a 7 percent coupon, the prime rate being 6 percent. Acme has enjoyed increased earnings for the last five years. In fact, its earnings have been growing at about 20 percent per year. The market-place has also valued its securities at a mean price-earnings ratio (*P/E*) of 15. What are the potential costs of such an issue, assuming a stable market and *P/E* over the next five years? There are two basic considerations: 1) the present value of all interest charges to be paid over the next five years; and 2) the present value of the future stock sale cost in terms of foregone capital. The present value of paying $350,000 per year in interest for five years at 20 percent (the firm's internal cost of capital) is $1,148,210. That is, this figure is the present value of the alternative uses of the $350,000 per year had it been employed elsewhere. Since earnings should grow at 20 percent per year, the common price in five years should be $112 since earnings will have grown to $7.46 per share from $3.00 and the *P/E* is assumed to remain at 15. The cost here is quite evident. Acme will be selling shares at $55 when it could have sold them for about $112. The difference, $57, must be considered a cost. The present value of $57 not received five years hence at 20 percent is $22.91 per share. Since 100,000 warrants are issued, the potential cost is $2,291,000. Thus the real cost of the issue is $3,-439,210, that is, the present value of all coupon payments plus the present value of a future discounted price on stock sales. How can the flexibility of the warrant alter the decision-making process? Quite simply. The issuer now asks the investment banker to bid on other combinations, varying the number of warrants, exercise price, and the bond coupon rate. By varying these factors, the issuing firm can, by going through considerable negotiation with the underwriter, find the most economical combination of financing. Such flexibility is possible only with the warrant. The above example is illustrative of a technique which becomes more sophisticated when allowances are made for possible change in earnings as well as the probability that holders will exercise warrants over time rather than hold them until expiration. However, the principles of evaluation remain the same.

Stock-warrant units are also enjoying increased use. This is most pronounced in the new issues market, although many established firms with a market for their common are using this type of offering. For new issues, the attachment of the warrant provides better marketability for the common, a greater price (cash intake), and more market interest than would have been possible without the warrant. It often allows the issuer to sell common at a higher price than would have been possible otherwise. The difference between the warrant market price and the unit offering price is usually greater than the price the common would have commanded by itself. More importantly, the marketplace tends to identify the stock price with the unit price, thus establishing a mental set about what the common is worth, which would usually be lower on a straight stock issue.

Established firms, since they are not coming to the public markets for the first time, often must sell their common below the current market price. This is due to the laws of supply and demand as well as to the fact that there is an immediate dilution in earnings that may or may not be recovered by the utilization of the capital raised. By attaching a warrant the firm is able to sell the common at market or slightly above. The psychological implications of this action cannot be over-emphasized. With low-priced issues ($10 or less) the attach-ment of a warrant is even more significant from a market price standpoint. The warrant provides downside protection to the issuer at a time when he most needs it.

Warrants are enjoying continued growth and variation by acquiring firms. This trend is quite significant in light of the current tax structure impediments that face the acquiring firm and the target shareholders. Most acquisitions are for stock only, whereby the acquiring company receives all the assets of the target company in the form of voting stock for a fixed number of shares of the acquiring company's stock. Such an exchange qualifies for a tax-free reorganization under Section 368 (a) (1) (C) of the Internal Revenue Code. Whenever nonvoting securities are exchanged for the target company's assets there is some question as to whether the exchange is in fact tax-free. Since warrants and convertible bonds are nonvoting securities, there is a real question as to their use in acquisitions. Occasionally Section 368 (a) (2) (B) of the code provides an out, since it allows "other property" in lieu of "solely voting stock" to be used in acquiring up to 20 percent of the object firm's assets. There is a real limitation on the use of this clause, however, since assumed liabilities are considered to be "other property" and there are not many firms existing today that would leave much room for warrants in that 20 percent after assumed liabilities are accounted for. Where assumed liabilities represent less than 20 percent of the value of a firm, warrants or other nonvoting securities may be used.

Warrant conversion privileges are valued higher in the marketplace than comparable privileges associated with other convertible instruments, especially the convertible bond. There are many reasons why warrants do and should enjoy this popularity. Many investors wish to purchase a pure, long-term option. The convertible bond requires substantial additional outlays to cover the debt portion of the instrument. Almost all convertible bonds have call provisions which are frequently utilized by the issuer; therefore, the potential purchaser of convertible bonds is taking a calculated risk that the issuer may call his bond. It is certain that the issuer will do this when it is to his own rather than to the holder's benefit. There are very few callable warrants issued and outstanding today. The fact that the convertible bond's price fluctuates inversely with prime interest rates, all other things being equal, also adds confusion to the problem of one looking primarily for an option. This has the effect of creating a fluctuating exercise price since a convertible bond is convertible into a fixed number of shares. As an example, a convertible bond selling at face and being convertible into 50 shares of common has an *exercise price* of $20. However, if a rise in interest rates lowers the market price to $750, then the exercise price is $15. Such fluctuations make option evaluation difficult. The problem is even more difficult if current yield and yield to maturity figures are evaluated along with the option feature, as should be done, to produce a present value for the instrument. The assignment of a probability distribution for the call feature over the life of the bond is a task that cannot be adequately accomplished. As a result, convertible bonds tend to be inadequately or improperly evaluated by the option seeker. The one major advantage that convertible bonds have is the more favorable margin requirements. However, as interest rates hover at one of the highest points in decades the advantage of buying on margin is suspect. This is clearly reflected in the periodic shrinking of margin amounts within the brokerage industry as interest rates rise.

FUTURE USES

As the nature of the warrant becomes more complex, so do its uses. Recently a couple of firms have declared warrant dividends. This action provides benefits to the shareholder as well as to the issuer. The shareholder suffers no immediate per share earnings dilution, receives a long-term call on the common, and has an opportunity to capture capital gains through exercise or sale. The issuer satisfies the need for a dividend, prevents immediate dilution, has no cash outflow problem associated with dividends, and generally enjoys those benefits previously discussed relative to the issuer of warrants. A warrant dividend is the only type of dividend that has the potential to return more cash to the business than was spent in paying the dividend. Fuqua Industries' announcement in 1969 of a changeover from cash to warrant-stock dividends had no apparent adverse effect on the price of the common. The immediate cash benefit to the firm is obvious. More and more firms will employ this form of dividend.

Warrants have been used for many years to compensate underwriters and promoters of new firms. This use is just now being extended to cover key employees previously covered by a qualified stock option program. It seems reasonable that a number of firms will replace stock option plans with warrant plans. The benefits are apparent. Recent tax rulings have taken much of the play out of stock option plans. Warrants allow the employer to set the exercise price wherever he wishes. Although the recipient must report the fair market value of warrants received minus purchase price as income in the year received, he can sell the warrants after six months, paying only capital gains taxes. Stock purchased under a qualified stock option plan must be held for three years before long-term capital gains can be taken. There is also a great advantage to warrants in that there may be a public market for such instruments; however, there is no such market for an employee stock option. An employee making $20,000 per year may very well have an option on $30,000 worth of stock, exercisable in three segments over a three-year option period. This implies that the employee, wishing to exercise his option, will have to produce $10,000 in cash per year for three years. In spite of the fact that employers and their banks have often "floated" this three-year program, sometimes in less than a legal manner, the reason for the cash outlay is obvious. A trading warrant, however, could be sold, exercised, or a little bit of both depending on the desires of the employee. The use of warrant option programs should flourish over the next five to ten years. At the end of this period the government will have learned the name of the game and the show will be over.

The disguised warrant is the newest form of security and should produce some interesting issues over the next few years. A very interesting development was the recent take over of Warner Brothers-Seven Arts by Warner Communications. Warner created a new class of series "C" preferred stock for the take-over. This preferred stock is, as was mentioned before, a bona fide warrant. It pays a meager dividend, five cents per share, and does have a straight convertible feature, being convertible into one sixteenth of a share of Warner common. An additional provision allows that the holder, if he wishes, may exchange the preferred and $37.00 cash for one share of Warner common up to July 8, 1979. That clause makes this issue a warrant. However, institutions that couldn't or wouldn't buy a Warner warrant may buy a preferred. It is quite an interesting issue and bodes well for future inventiveness.

These and other developments suggest that common stock warrants will enjoy wider use and acceptance. The time lag between financial innovation and tax reform serves as an impetus for a steady stream of variations on the conversion theme.

3

Leverage and Some Other Relevant Concepts

T HE MAIN REASON why people purchase warrants is leverage—this is what warrant buying is all about.

LEVERAGE

The characteristic known as leverage is a much sought after and often little understood aspect of warrant investing. The term means exactly what it implies; that is, warrants tend to move more dramatically than the optioned stock. This works on both the upside as well as the downside. If a warrant moves up 30 percent on a 10 percent price increase in the stock, then the warrant has leverage in relation to the stock. In this example it is called "leverage of 3" or "3 to 1 leverage." Sometimes this is called the *leverage ratio*. Figure 3–1 illustrates leverage ratios which are expressed as the percentage increase in the price of the warrant divided by the percentage increase in the price of the stock.

54

These figures are not really meaningful because warrants do not always sell in a fixed relationship with the stock. For instance, when the stock sells far above the exercise price, as five or ten times as much, experienced leverage ratios tend to be much smaller than they were at lower stock prices. Just because a warrant demonstrates a leverage ratio of five when the stock moves from $10 to $20 does not mean it will

FIGURE 3–1
Leverage Ratios

Increase in Stock Price (percentage)	*Increase in Warrant Price (percentage)*	*Leverage Ratio*
100	200	2.0
200	300	1.5
500	1,500	3.0
1,000	5,000	5.0

perform in a like manner for the move from $20 to $40. Take a look at leverage in action. Figure 3–2 illustrates the price experience of Continental Telephone (CTC) for one year.

Do not let the lines themselves fool you. Remember, the common is shown on a scale of about $21, whereas the warrant is on a scale of about $7. When illustrated on semi-log paper, the percentage price swings are clearly shown, as illustrated in Figure 3–3. The grid of the chart is constructed so that equal percentage price changes are properly reflected in the vertical movement of the line.

Without any fancy mathematics it is clear that CTC common moved from a low of $18.63 to a high of $26.00 in a matter of about seven months. This represents a price gain of $7.37, or 39.5 percent. During the same period the warrant

FIGURE 3–2
Continental Telephone (CTC)

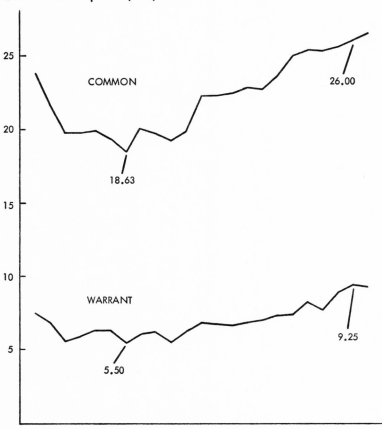

COMMON

26.00

18.63

WARRANT

9.25

5.50

BI-WEEKLY PRICES 4/70 THROUGH 3/71

moved from $5.50 to $9.25, an increase of $3.75, or 68.2 percent. Clearly, the warrant moved almost twice as quickly as the common and therefore has leverage in relation to the common. This leverage may not appear to be spectacular, but, when weighed against the risks of a utility-type firm, such as CTC, it must be considered very good. Of course there are examples of astounding leverage in action. Many years ago

FIGURE 3–3

Continental Telephone (bi-weekly prices April 1970–March 1971 on semi-log scale)

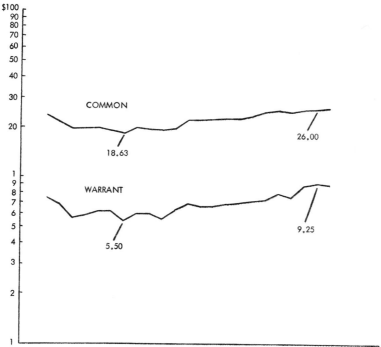

Tri-Continental's warrant moved in a spectacular fashion in relation to the stock. A little-known silver mining firm, Agau Mines, had a warrant that made a momentous move in a short span of ten months during 1969–70. Specifically, in the summer of 1969 the stock was around 63 cents while the warrant (a call on one share of common at 63 cents) sold at 17 cents. By April of 1970 the stock had moved to $7.25, not bad in its own right—a move of slightly over 1,000 percent. However, the warrant stood at $6.25, a move of 3,677 percent! Nevertheless the percentage move in the warrant was much

FIGURE 3–4
Stock/Warrant Price Relationships

These warrants easily outpaced their common share partners...

	Warrants			Common		
	Recent price	Price May 29/70	Change — % —	Recent price	Price May 29/70	Change — % —
Rothmans of Pall Mall Canada Ltd. .	3.00	1.35	+122	13	10 ¼	+27
Husky Oil Ltd.	6.75	3.10	+118	12 ¾	8 ¾	+46
Jefferson Lake Petrochem. of Cda. Ltd.	3.40	1.60	+113	10 ¼	9	+14
Gaz Métropoltain Inc. (1966 wts.) .	1.85	0.90	+106	5	3.80	+32
Markborough Properties Ltd.	1.70	0.89	+91	5 ¼	3	+75
TransCanada PipeLines Ltd.	11.50	6.55	+76	32	24 ¾	+29
Shell Investments Ltd. ....'.	15.00	9.20	+63	30 ⅛	24 ⅛	+25
Atlantic Sugar Refineries Co.	2.10	1.30	+62	7	6	+17
Northern & Central Gas Corp.	6.80	4.20	+62	13 ⅞	10 ¾	+29
Interprovincial Pipe Line Co. ~......	12.50	7.75	+61	24 ⅝	19	+30
Industrial Acceptance Corp.	5.50	3.55	+55	15 ⅛	12 ¼	+23
Famous Players Cdn. Corp.	1.50	1.00	+50	9 ½	9 ¼	+3
Imperial General Properties Ltd.	0.75	0.50	+50	2.80	2.25	+24

...but there were declines, too

Consolidated-Bathurst Ltd. (1968 wts.)	3.05	5.50	—45	15 ½	16 ½	—6
Acres Ltd.	1.50	2.65	—43	6 ⅝	10 ¾	—38
Belding Corticelli Ltd.	1.75	2.65	—34	8	9 ½	—16
Glengair Group Ltd.	0.90	1.35	—33	2	2.90	—31
E-L Financial Corp.	1.85	2.00	—8	6 ¼	5 ½	+14
Canadian Pacific Investments Ltd. ...	4.90	5.05	—3	23 ¼	23 ⅜	—1

Source: *The Financial Post,* December 24, 1970, p. 28.

greater at the lower end of the common range than at the higher.

In October of 1970 *The Financial Post,* the *Barron's* of Canada, published a table as illustrated in Figure 3–4. This table represents price changes over a mere 4½ month period. Of course, the period spanned a significant market rise from the May 1970 low of the Dow (632) to a recovery level of the Dow (759) on October 23, 1970. However, the power of leverage is quite evident in the percentage changes shown for corresponding stocks and warrants.

Another and slightly more appropriate measure of leverage

is called the *leverage indicator*. This is derived by merely dividing the stock price by the warrant price, adjusted if needed to reflect the cost of a call on one full share. If a warrant trades at $6 when the stock is $18, then the leverage indicator is 3.0. If the warrant is $10 and the stock is $15, then the leverage indicator is 1.5. This measure has a limited use in comparing warrants. It is not practical to assume that when the leverage indicator is 2.5 the warrant will move two and one half times as much as the stock, percentagewise. It just doesn't happen that way. It is fair to say, however, that a high leverage indicator (more than 2.0) signifies that a warrant may be attractive and as such should be carefully evaluated. At best the leverage indicator is a relative measure and should be used only in conjunction with other analytical tools. The leverage indicator is merely a hint that a warrant may be desirable.

When you buy stock on margin you experience leverage— that is, you have more dollars working for you than you had to put up. If you put up 50 percent margin to buy and the stock doubles, then you have enjoyed leverage in relation to the other fellow who put up the full cost. Some people believe the shares of closed-end investment trusts represent a leveraged call on the future of the economy. Since many trusts periodically sell below net asset value it is possible to get more than one dollar working for you when you invest. This is a form of leverage. It would seem reasonable to assume that a warrant which calls an investment trust share (selling below net asset value) possesses double leverage, or, leverage on leverage. In the past, as with Tri-Continental, this has been true. However, in recent years closed-end investment trust warrants have not enjoyed the same action as in the past. Large dividends and capital gains distributions made to shareholders (but not to warrantholders of course) have kept share price growth down and hence warrant values down.

The ultimate for the leverage addict is a call option on a warrant. That is, the purchase of an option which gives the right to purchase a warrant, which in turn is the right to purchase stock. This is truly leverage on leverage and can result in dramatic gains. A discussion of calls, which are high risk instruments designed for professional traders, is beyond the scope of this book. The fact that only about 20 percent of all calls written are exercised suggests that 80 percent of the time the purchaser is left with some wallpaper and a nice tax loss.

INTRINSIC VALUE

Since a warrant is merely an option to buy stock, it should never sell at more than the stock price, as long as it is a call on one share of stock. Suppose that a warrant represents the right to buy one share of a stock selling at $10. No one knowing the warrant terms would pay $11 for the warrant when the stock could be purchased at $10. The practical upper limit on any warrant price is the optioned stock price. The value of all warrants consists of two distinct parts: intrinsic value (sometimes called tangible value) and premium. When the optioned stock sells above the warrant exercise price, the difference between the stock price and the exercise price is the intrinsic value. When the optioned stock sells below the warrant exercise price, the warrant has no intrinsic value; in fact, it can be considered to have negative intrinsic value. To illustrate, assume that a warrant calls one share of stock at $6 per share. The stock sells at $10 and the warrant is at $8. Here the intrinsic value is clearly $10 less $6, or

$4. This is how much the warrant is worth upon immediate exercise (conversion). One could surrender his warrant certificate along with $6 in cash and receive one share of stock which in turn could be sold for $10. The net value of this operation is $4, or the warrant's intrinsic value. Suppose the same warrant sold at $3 while the stock stood at $5. Here the intrinsic value is $5 less $6, or a negative $1. What this means is that the stock must move up $1 in order for the warrant to have an intrinsic value of zero. Many stocks sell far below the warrant exercise price, suggesting that the warrant may never again possess intrinsic value.

The intrinsic value of a warrant sets a lower limit on a warrant's market price. Clearly, if a warrant sold for less than its intrinsic value, it would be worthwhile to buy warrants, exercise them, and sell the obtained stock. Arbitrageurs make a living by keeping the market price of warrants and other convertibles at least in line with intrinsic value. Arbitrage is the process of simultaneously buying and selling the same or equivalent securities in order to profit from a price discrepancy. A simple example is the simultaneous purchase of A.T.&T. stock on the New York Stock Exchange and its sale on the Pacific Coast Exchange because there is a price discrepancy. Professional traders insure that the spread on A.T.&T., during the hours when both exchanges are open, is at minimum. Those who pay regular commissions cannot afford to play this game—there just isn't enough of a spread. However, in convertible securities, a small spread between values sometimes develops. Occasionally a warrant will sell for slightly less than intrinsic value. In recent years this has never been more than a few percentage points below, like 3 percent to 5 percent below intrinsic value. Only the specialists and professionals, working on little or no commissions and high volume, can profit from these discrepancies in the auction markets. From a practical point of view it is safe to assume that a warrant never sells below intrinsic value.

Based on the simple analysis of common sense about option

FIGURE 3–5
Minimum and Maximum Warrant Prices

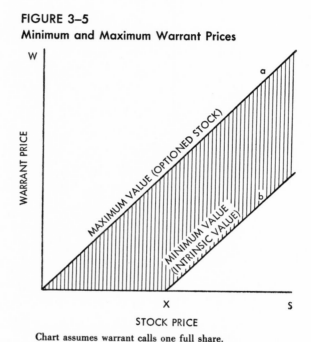

Chart assumes warrant calls one full share.

prices described above, it is easy to set an upper limit (optioned stock price) and a lower limit (intrinsic value) for the market price of a warrant, as Figure 3–5 illustrates.

Line *a* depicts the upper limit for the warrant price as the 45° angle from the axis suggests. All along line *a*, for all stock prices, the warrant price is equal to the stock price. This is the maximum possible price for the warrant. Line *b* emanates from the point *X*, which represents the warrant exercise price.

Line *b* describes the minimum value for a warrant since all points on that line represent the intrinsic value for the corresponding stock price. Clearly, a warrant must sell somewhere within the shaded area.

PREMIUM

Not all warrants sell at intrinsic value; in fact, very few actually do and, when they do, it is not for too long. Warrant investors pay premiums for leverage; that is, in the hope of participating in an upward warrant price change that far ·exceeds that of the optioned stock. Most warrants sell at substantial premiums, suggesting that investors are willing to assume some risks in order to participate in a potentially greater reward.

Warrant premiums are computed measures that assist in comparing the relative merits of warrant issues. Before an accurate comparison can be made, all warrants must be observed as a call on one share of stock. Suppose that a warrant trades as a call on 1.5 shares of stock with an exercise price of $5.20 per share. The stock sells at $8.00 and the warrant at $7.50. The adjusted warrant price is $7.50/1.5, or $5.00. Thus an option on one share of stock at $5.20 costs $5.00. The warrant's intrinsic value is the stock price less the effective exercise price per share, or $8.00 less $5.20 giving $2.80. This is the immediate worth of the option on one share of stock. The adjusted warrant price must be at least $2.80, or arbitrageurs would simultaneously buy warrants and sell stock short, using the stock obtained through warrant exercise to cover the short position.

A premium results when a warrant sells at an adjusted warrant price (or market price if it is a call on one share of stock) that is greater than its intrinsic value. The premium is the adjusted warrant price less its intrinsic value. A percent premium is computed when the premium amount is divided by the stock price. Let us assume that a warrant is a call on one share of stock at $25, that there is no bond usable at face, and that the stock and warrant market prices are $30 and $15 respectively. The intrinsic value is $30 less $25, or $5. The premium is $15 less $5, or $10. The percent premium is $10/$30, or 33 percent. In the previous example, where the intrinsic value was $2.80, the premium is $5.00 less $2.80 giving $2.20. The percent premium is $2.20/$8.00, or 27½ percent. Now there is a basis for comparison which was not immediately ascertainable by observing the market prices of the individual warrant and stock issues.

When the market price of the stock is below the effective per share exercise price, there are differing opinions as to how the premium should be computed. Some analysts, choosing to disguise the excessive premiums paid for some warrants, use a less conservative method which fails to recognize negative intrinsic values. Consider that the market price of the previously cited warrant (with an exercise price of $25) drops to $8 as a result of the stock price dropping to $20. The less conservative technique calculates a new percent premium as $8 less $0 divided by $20 giving 40 percent. An analyst recognizing negative intrinsic values would calculate the new percent premium at $8 less a negative $5 for a total of $13 divided by $20 giving 65 percent. This method always results in a percent premium which is equal to the percentage by which the stock price must advance in order that the warrant's intrinsic value becomes equal to the warrant's current market price. In the example this means that the stock, now at $20, would have to rise 65 percent to $33 in order for the warrant to have an intrinsic value of $8. It should be clear that a premium expressed in absolute dollars is of no use for comparative purposes, for warrants with different exercise prices could never be compared. However, when premiums are expressed as a percentage of the stock price as described above, comparison between warrants becomes meaningful.

Leverage and premium together begin to form a basis for warrant analysis. The typical investor seeks high leverage at a low premium. Highly leveraged warrants are usually a call on a stock that is selling well below the exercise price. As an example, a warrant may be a call on one share at $55 when the stock is at $20. The warrant might sell for as little as $5, giving a leverage indicator of 4.0. However, the premium is an excessive 200 percent. It is very difficult to find an actively traded warrant with a few years to go before expiration selling at a large leverage indicator and at a low premium.

Recall that investors pay more than intrinsic value for a warrant in the hope of participating in a price upswing before warrant expiration. As the expiration date nears, the chances that the stock will move significantly within time diminish. In fact, who would pay more than intrinsic value for a warrant the day before its scheduled expiration? How much was it worth a week before? One month? Three months? The facts are that a warrant is worth and sells for little more than intrinsic value in its waning months. During these months the leverage indicator may go sky high, like up to 100 or more. In terms of Figure 3–5 a warrant must approach line *b* upon expiration. Suppose a stock sells at the exercise price of $55. During the last few weeks the warrant might sell for $1.00 or less. Leverage is clearly high and the premium is negligible. However, approaching expiration explains why this otherwise opportune possibility is a mirage.

VOLATILITY

Warrant price swings tend to be more pronounced than those of the underlying stock. A measure of such price swings is called a *volatility gauge.* One way of measuring this is to divide the difference between the high and low of a security over a period of time by its average price. In Figure 3–2 CTC common has a volatility measure of ($26.00 − 18.63)/[(26.00 + 18.63)/2] or 0.33, while the warrant's measure is ($9.25 − 5.50)/[(9.25 + 5.50)/2] or 0.51. These numbers are sometimes expressed in terms of 33 percent and 51 percent. It is important when comparing volatility measures that they be computed over the same period of time. In the above example this is less than one year. Since high-low data are easily obtained for the last 12 months, this is a typically used period.

ADJUSTED WARRANT

One of the most important aspects of warrant trading is the ability to select from a host of investment alternatives. Such a selection requires the ability to perform comparative analysis. If all warrants had the same basic terms, that is, all were a call on one share at the same exercise price for the same period of time, then analysis would be easy. It would be quite simple to chart, over time, the price relationships on a diagram like the previously discussed Figure 3–5. However, it is probably fortunate from an opportunity-to-profit angle that warrants are not alike and therefore a method for evaluation must be found. The process of rendering a warrant so that it may be adequately compared to others from a technical point of view is called creating an "adjusted," "normalized," or "relative" warrant. First, the warrant price must be adjusted so that it represents a call on one share of stock. Suppose a warrant calls 1.5 shares of common at $25 per share and the warrant sells at $25 while the stock is at $40 and a usable bond is at $90. Since the exercise price is expressed in "per share" terms, no adjustment is required. However an *adjusted warrant price* is obtained by dividing the warrant price ($25) by the shares optioned (1.5) giving $16.67. This adjusted warrant price reflects the cost of an option on one share. The exercise price must also be adjusted to reflect the usable bond as discussed in Chapter 1. The adjusted exercise price is clearly 90 percent of $25, or $22.50. Now we have an *adjusted warrant;* that is, we have transformed its natural terms and market prices into adjusted terms and market prices as if it were a call on one share of stock. The same technique must be applied to all other warrants to be compared which do not naturally fall into the adjusted warrant form. Fortunately most warrants are a call on one whole share at a specified per share exercise price and do not have usable bonds to be considered. Only about 15 percent of the warrants outstanding need to be transformed in this manner. However, the job is only half done. We still need to adjust for the fact that warrants have different exercise prices. The warrants to be compared must be transformed to account for the differences in effective per share exercise prices. This is accomplished by dividing the observed adjusted warrant price by the per share exercise price to create a *relative warrant price* (W/E). At the same time the stock price is divided by the per share exercise price to create a *relative stock price* (S/E). Thus the adjusted warrant prices and the optioned stock prices are expressed as percentages of the per share exercise price. Now Figure 3–5 can be made much more useful, as shown in Figure 3–6.

Now it is possible to plot different warrants with their unique terms and obtain a comparative picture. In Figure 3–6 this has been done for two warrants for the periods shown in Figure 3–7.

As shown in Figure 3–6, the cluster of points for Elgin

FIGURE 3–6
Comparison for Elgin (ENW) and Continental Telephone (CTC)

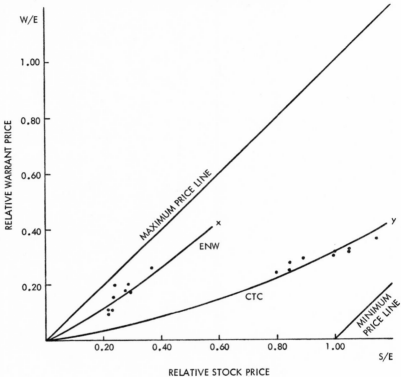

RELATIVE STOCK PRICE

(ENW) is much closer to the maximum price line than is the cluster of points for Continental Telephone (CTC).

The two lines (*x* and *y*) emanating from the origin pass through the center of the two respective clusters. These two lines would approximate the center line for the lifetime cluster for each warrant, had we gone to the trouble to plot them. What does this mean? It is visibly evident that line *x*, representing ENW, is much higher in the zone of possible price relationships than is line *y*, representing CTC. This suggests that investors have been willing to pay more for the ENW

FIGURE 3–7

Elgin National Industries (ENW)

	Stock	Warrant	Per Share Exercise Price	Adjusted Warrant Price	W/E	S/E
4/3/70	$8.13	$2.25	$21.88	$5.63	0.257	0.372
5/1/70	6.38	1.75	"	4.38	0.200	0.292
5/29/70	6.13	1.63	"	4.08	0.186	0.280
6/26/70	5.38	1.75	"	4.38	0.200	0.246
7/24/70	5.38	1.38	"	3.45	0.158	0.246
8/21/70	5.13	1.25	"	3.13	0.143	0.234
9/18/70	6.25	1.50	"	3.75	0.171	0.286
10/16/70	6.13	1.63	"	4.08	0.186	0.280
11/13/70	5.25	1.38	"	3.45	0.158	0.240
12/11/70	5.13	1.38	"	3.45	0.158	0.234

ENW calls 0.4 shares at 21.88 per share.

Continental Telephone (CTC)

	Stock	Warrant	Per Share Exercise Price	Adjusted Warrant Price	W/E	S/E
4/3/70	$23.75	$7.50	$22.38	$7.50	0.335	1.06
5/1/70	19.75	5.63	"	5.63	0.252	0.88
5/29/70	19.88	6.25	"	6.25	0.279	0.89
6/26/70	18.63	5.50	"	5.50	0.246	0.83
7/24/70	19.75	6.13	"	6.13	0.274	0.88
8/21/70	19.88	6.25	"	6.25	0.279	0.89
9/18/70	22.25	6.75	"	6.75	0.302	0.99
10/16/70	22.88	6.88	"	6.88	0.307	1.02
11/13/70	23.63	7.25	"	7.25	0.324	1.06
12/11/70	25.38	8.13	"	8.13	0.363	1.13

CTC calls 1.0 shares at 22.38 per share.

warrant than they have for CTC's. Or, to be more precise, the ENW warrant has enjoyed a richer price and more healthy premium than CTC. This chart does not tell us *why* the ENW warrant is more expensive than CTC's; it just illustrates that it is. This fact was not clearly evident by looking at the prices for the two issues. By creating the *W/E* and *S/E* figures it is possible to compare graphically any number of issues. What is left is the development of a norm against which these individual warrant curves can be compared. That is, it is possible to illustrate on graphs a normal curve of all warrants as is discussed in the next chapter.

Occasionally a reference is made to the fact that a warrant is selling at *parity*. This happens when the optioned stock price is at the effective exercise price. In terms of Figure 3–6 it is when *S/E* equals 1.0 or when the stock price is 100 percent of the effective exercise price. If CTC stock sold at $22.38, then the warrant would be selling at parity. At this point the CTC warrant might sell for $7 or so.

All references to warrants in the future will be in terms of an "adjusted warrant."

4

Price Determination

THE ULTIMATE OBJECTIVE of any form of security analysis, either fundamental or technical, is to find out whether a given security is overpriced or underpriced, or just fairly valued by the marketplace. Of course a security, like any other salable item, is only worth as much as someone is willing to pay for it. In the stock market it is the interaction of the buyers and sellers through their bid and asked prices that determines price. Therefore people value securities and set the price. In the field of warrants, price is composed of two parts: intrinsic value and premium. The rationale for the intrinsic value segment is quite simple: Arbitrage insures that there is an honest and close appraisal here. However, there are a host of things that investors consider when establishing a premium for a warrant. Statistically there is a relationship between stock price and premium. Figure 4–1 illustrates this relationship as rendered by the Investment Bankers Association (IBA) in a special study commissioned by the Internal Revenue Service.

What this tells us is that on the average people are willing to pay a 41 percent premium for a typical warrant with at least two years of life remaining, when the stock is at 100 percent of the exercise price and as a result the intrinsic value is zero. As an example, suppose a warrant calls one share at $50 and this is where the stock now sits. The typical warrant

FIGURE 4–1
Warrant Premiums

Stock Price as Percent of Exercise Price	Warrant Price as Percent of Exercise Price
80%	28%
90	34
100	41
110	48
120	55

Source: Investment Bankers Association of America. *Federal Income Taxation of Compensatory Options (incluing Warrants) Granted to Underwriters and Other Independent Contractors* (1963), p. 39.

might sell at 41 percent of $50, or $20.50. Since the warrant has no intrinsic value this warrant price must be all premium. If the same stock sold at $40, then the typical warrant might sell at 28 percent of $50, or $14. Again, this is all premium. Should the stock sell at 120 percent of the exercise price, that is, at $60, then the warrant might sell for 55 percent of $50, or $27.50. Here $10 of this warrant price is intrinsic value and $17.50 is premium. Of course, these numbers are averages and do not really tell us much about specific warrants. What we are really concerned with are those factors which investors consider when establishing these warrant premiums for specific issues.

OPTIONED STOCK PRICE

The most significant determinant of a warrant's price is the value of the optioned stock. At a minimum investors will pay the warrant's intrinsic value. A warrant that calls one share of stock at $22 might sell for $9 when the stock is at $25, giving the warrant $3 of intrinsic value and a $6 premium. What happens if the stock moves to $50? The warrant must at least move to $28, its new intrinsic value. In fact, it would probably sell for a little more than $28, assuming it had some time to go before expiration. Obviously the price of optioned stock has a great influence on the warrant's market price. This is the one determinant which is easily and objectively evaluated. Knowing the warrant terms and stock price, you can easily compute the intrinsic value of the warrant which is the minimum you should be willing to pay for the warrant.

EXPECTATIONS FOR OPTIONED STOCK

Warrants generally sell at a premium over intrinsic value because investors have positive notions about the prospects for the underlying stock. The greater these expectations, the greater will be the warrant premium. Thus the *expected value* of a warrant can be greater than its current price and it is very much determined by the expected value of the optioned stock. As a rule, investor expectations for a company are expressed in the price-earnings (*P/E*) ratio they are willing to pay. A firm which has been or appears ready to become an outstanding performer in its industry is generally accorded a relatively high *P/E*. As a rule, if the same firm has a warrant outstanding, investors are willing to pay more for it than other, more lackluster items.

Part of an investor's expectations for a company involves an evaluation of risk. A high *P/E* is sometimes indicative of a large downside risk. Impending or threatened legislation against an industry imparts an element of risk. If a firm has a large overseas investment there are certain risks, such as repatriation of assets by a foreign power, tariff changes, or investment restrictions. Since most investors are risk avoiders, the expectation of risk usually places a dampening effect on market prices. Thus, there are a number of factors which go into the typical investor's formulation of an expected future value for the optioned stock. It is not the intent here to discuss the aspects of fundamental security analysis. Volumes have been written on this art over the years. It is significant to note that investors do not discount the same thing twice. Therefore, although *P/E*s and risk factors are significant in determining the price of optioned stock, it is the stock price and not the underlying factors that determines warrant prices from a technical point of view. Since the stock price has already discounted projected future earnings or the lack of them, there is no real correlation between earnings and warrant prices. Instead, the correlation is to stock price, both present and expected.

LENGTH OF CALL

Except for a few warrants which are perpetual, there is an end date (expiration date) when the warrant option ceases. When this date is far off (two or more years away) investors are willing to pay more, all other things being equal, for a warrant than when the date is close (weeks or months away). Investors are willing to pay a premium for a warrant that still has time to perform. As expiration nears, the amount of premium drops in an orderly fashion so that the final market price is usually the intrinsic value. Suppose a warrant calls one share of common at $15 and the stock goes for $20. If the warrant expires tomorrow what would we be willing to pay? Hopefully nothing more than the intrinsic value of $5. What if the warrant expires next week? Next month? Next year? Five years from now?

The facts are that an investor's horizon is quite limited. Although it seems logical that a ten-year call should be worth more than a three-year call on the same stock at the same price, it just is not valued that way in the market. Investors will not pay any more for the longer call. This was aptly illustrated in Figure 1–1 by the price action of the two McCrory warrants.

The IBA study referred in Figure 4–1 included an evaluation of when approaching expiration begins to affect the premiums investors are willing to pay. The standard premiums shown in Figure 4–2 are those implied in Figure 4–1.

Recall that based on Figure 4–1 investors might pay 41 percent of a $50 exercise price or $20.50 for a warrant whose stock sells at the exercise price. Based on Figure 4–2 investors would be willing to do this until the warrant has 26 months to go before expiration. At this point the standard premium begins to get cut until it is zero just before expiration. By interpolating on the graph, we find that when the warrant has nine months to go we might expect it to sell at about 28 percent of the standard premium, or $5.74 in our case.

This adjustment in premiums paid begins at about the three-year point, but becomes significant when the warrant hits the 26-month level. From a practical point of view you could consider that at two years the premium really begins to get chopped. An easy and fairly accurate way to calculate how much premium is lost is to assume that the relationship is a straight line and reduce the premium accordingly. As an example, the standard premium for the warrant we have been discussing is $20.50. When the warrant has 17 months to go we could calculate expected premium as $20.50 times

FIGURE 4–2

Analysis of Effect of Approaching Expiration (median percentage of standard premiums at which warrants were valued by the market, by number of months to expiration)

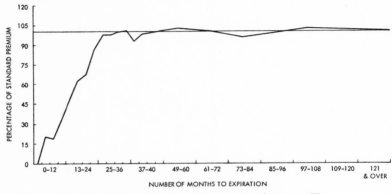

Source: IBA, *Federal Income Taxation of Compensatory Options,* p. 55.

17/24, or $14.52. At two months before expiration it would be worth 2/24ths of $20.50, or $1.71.

DIVIDENDS

One of the things that a warrantholder gives up is the right to participate in dividend distributions on the optioned stock. Looking at it in another way, the holder of stock enjoys dividend distributions (or at least the prospect of future distributions) while the warrantholder does not. By purchasing the warrant instead of the stock one forgoes these cash flows. Should the dividend rate be high, then the warrant becomes less valuable relative to the stock than it would be in the case of a little or no dividend. If there were two identical warrants trading as options on two different but equally priced shares of stock with the same prospects for growth, then the warrant on the stock with the higher dividend would trade at a lower price. This fact is best illustrated when a firm abruptly raises the dividend. As a rule, there is an immediate correction in the warrant on the downside. This seems reasonable since present dividends and the prospect of future dividends do have a value. The greater that value, the more desirable is the stock. In fact, there is a school of security analysis that suggests that the actual value (theoretical, not market) of a security should be computed as the present value of all future income streams (dividends and other distributions). Thus, it is suggested that "growth" stocks sell at high P/Es not because of anticipated growth in earnings, but because of anticipated dividends when the firm becomes "mature."

LISTING OF WARRANT

As a rule listed warrants are more valued by the marketplace than unlisted ones (all other things being equal). The reasons are the same as those that control the differential in value between two otherwise equal stocks, one being listed, the other not listed. The two major advantages of listed securities are liquidity and marginability.

The nation's exchanges still provide the most liquid markets, in spite of the great strides in the OTC markets due to the advent of NASDAQ (National Association of Securities Dealers Automated Quotation system), a computerized method of illustrating bid and asked prices. The best definition of liquidity from the warrantholder's point of view is a narrow spread between bid and asked prices and stability; that is, the market must be able to absorb a reasonable supply without having the prices fall out of bed. The major exchanges have listing requirements that are conducive to a liquid market. Typical requirements include minimums for such things as number of shares (warrants) outstanding, number of holders, corporate sales, earnings, assets, net worth, and the like. As a result, the warrants of the larger, better financed concerns which are also more widely held are listed. The mere announcement that a listing has been applied for usually results in an upward move in the warrant's market price.

As a rule, unlisted securities cannot be bought on margin. When a security is bought on margin, less than the full purchase price is paid and the remainder is borrowed, usually from the broker. If margin requirements are 55 percent, then you need put up only 55 percent of the purchase price. Therefore there is a kind of leverage in listed securities vis-à-vis unlisted ones in that it is possible to have more money working for you than is actually invested. Of course "invested" must be distinguished from "risked." With or without margin, risked (full) capital is the same. Listed securities are also useful as collateral when an investor is borrowing, which he can do directly in the margin account. It is possible to place listed securities in your margin account and then borrow against them to purchase additional securities. The exception to the rule on a listing is a small group of, at present, about 500 OTC issues on the "approved list" of the Federal Reserve Board. The securities on the list can be margined just like listed securities and therefore enjoy the added value they would have if they were listed. However, warrants do not appear on this list (this list is available from the Federal Reserve Bank in New York City).

USABLE SENIOR SECURITIES

You will recall that the existence of senior securities usable at face for exercise purposes may result in a lower effective per share exercise price. If a warrant calls one share at $20 and there is a usable bond selling at $800 (80 percent of face), then the effective exercise price is $16. You could go into the market, buy the bond at "80" ($800) and use it at face value, usually "100" ($1,000). As long as there is a senior security usable at and selling below face, the warrant price will tend to be higher than it might otherwise be.

The usable bonds should be carefully evaluated. There are cases where the advantages of such bonds are questionable. First of all, we might ask whether the bond is listed. If it is, there is probably a viable market. If it trades OTC, how active is it? Are the quoted prices obtainable? There are several examples where there is only an asked or bid price for an OTC bond. As a rule, this means there is no active market and the bond's usability should be completely discounted. When there is a large spread between the bid and asked prices, then the depth of the market is questionable.

When a broker quotes a large spread it is normally an attempt on his part to create or eliminate a position of his own at profitable prices. If you call on his side of the market and you are willing to pay the price, fine; he will fill your order. If you are on the other side, then the demand or supply just dried up. Some bonds become usable or cease being usable during the life of the warrant. The terms of usability should be carefully checked. The bond itself may be redeemable; in the event of this happening, its usability ends. If the usable bond is selling well below face because of serious financial problems, then there is a chance that it might rise in price (to the detriment of warrantholders) given an upturn in the fortunes of the company. Of course you would hope that as the debt price rose, so would the stock underlying the warrant, and any loss due to a higher effective per share exercise price would be more than offset by the resultant increase in the warrant's intrinsic value.

Another significant factor is the percentage of the bonds outstanding that would be required to exercise the entire warrant issue. In some cases there are not even enough bonds outstanding to exercise the entire warrant issue. In these cases the bonds' usability is suspect. This is most significant if a warrant, with an insufficient supply of usable bonds, were callable and in fact was called by the issuer. In this event there would be a mad dash for the usable bonds and any discount from face the bonds had would soon be eliminated by the very strong rules of supply and demand.

The effect of a usable bond should be considered only when its marketability is unquestioned and its usability is expected to continue over the life of the warrant.

VOLATILITY

Another factor that warrant investors consider in setting the price of a warrant is the volatility of the underlying stock. Volatility is a measure of the magnitude of historical price changes. A highly volatile stock is one that experiences wide percentage price swings. One measure of volatility, as previously discussed, would be the difference between an issue's high and low price divided by the average price over the same period of time.

There are a number of similar ways of measuring this factor of volatility, but the principle is the same. Investors value warrants that call highly volatile stocks because they feel that these stocks have a higher probability (all other things being equal) of going up more dramatically than others. For this possible display of fireworks warrant investors are willing to pay a premium.

EXISTENCE OF OTHER CONVERTIBLES

If a company has other convertible securities outstanding which pay high dividends, then their effect is quite similar to that of a high dividend on the underlying stock. This is most significant when the other convertible is selling at a small premium so that the buyer can achieve a high yield and at the same time enjoy the same type of conversion privilege as the warrantholders. The existence of such securities, priced at a low premium, usually is a depressant on the warrant price.

STEPS IN EXERCISE PRICE

The existence of steps in the exercise price over the life of the warrant tends to reduce the option's value. The more steps there are, or the larger a step, the lesser the value. The marketplace begins to discount a step-up in exercise price about 15 months before it happens. Thus you could prorate the expected increase over the 15-month period and at any given point in time calculate "the market's" exercise price. Of course the issuer's intent is clear; it hopes it will not be selling stock too much below the market in the future. However, large steps have in the past backfired. In a few cases the effect has been a large conversion of warrants just before the step, resulting in the sale of stock at the price which the step was attempting to avoid. If the step had been reasonable (10 percent instead of 30 percent or more), then wholesale conversion may have been avoided.

CONSTRAINTS ON WARRANT

Warrants are often issued in a *nondetachable* or *nonexercisable* form. When warrants are issued in a unit, as with stock or bonds, they are quite often not detachable (or, as it is sometimes stated, "not separately transferable") for a period of time, typically 30 to 90 days. As a rule, a "when detached" market develops in these securities and there is no problem trading in them. However, it is impossible to take delivery until after the detachable date. This nontransferability in the early life of the warrant hinders the issue's liquidity, and as such has a dampening effect on the warrant price. However, this effect is minimal.

More important than deferred transferability is the subject of deferred exercisability. Quite often warrants are issued and are not exercisable for many months, in some cases even years. The longer the period of nonexercisability, the more detrimental is the effect on the current warrant price. Although warrants are bought to be sold, not exercised, it is nice to know that they can be exercised at the holder's desire. If a warrant, selling at a small premium, called a stock upon which a stock distribution was about to be made (as in a spin-off) and the warrantholders could not participate due to the antidilution provisions, then it might be nice to convert and participate before the distribution record date (the day for determining shareholders of record who are eligible for distributions). Of course there is usually an appropriate price drop the day the stock goes "ex dividend."

There are a host of other reasons why warrantholders might like to be able to exercise their options. Suppose you own warrants which call Big Promise, Inc., and along comes Better Promise, Inc. with a tender offer for Big Promise offering 30 percent above the market for the stock. At this point there may be no mention of the warrants in the tender. This would be especially true if Better Promise were after less than 100 percent of Big Promise's stock. At this point you might like to exercise and tender. For these and many other reasons a nonexercisable clause tends to reduce the price investors are willing to pay for different warrants of otherwise equivalent value.

CALL ON OTHER THAN COMMON

Some warrants are a call on a security other than common stock. As an example a warrant might call a preferred stock instead of the common. Since preferreds tend to be "money rate" stocks (that is, their market price is more closely correlated with interest rates than it is with the fortunes of the issuer), the volatility of preferreds is lower than that of the corresponding common. As a result, all other things being equal, a warrant which calls a preferred is less valuable than one that calls common. This is reasonable, since a great increase in earnings usually results in a corresponding movement in the common stock, but may result in little or no change in a preferred (unless it is also convertible into common). Other things, such as the ability to pay dividends, are more important to the preferred shareholder. As a rule, warrants which call a security other than common stock offer limited potential.

Occasionally a warrant calls a package of securities. This happens when there are mergers, distributions, and other corporate capital structure changes which result in appropriate changes to the terms of the warrant due to implementation of antidilution provisions. One of the better known warrants that had such terms was the Hilton Hotel warrant which expired in 1971. As a result of a number of capital structure changes, this warrant was a call on the following package of securities: (*a*) 2.0 shares of Hilton common, (*b*) 0.144375 share of TWA common, and (*c*) 0.2625 share of TWA series 'A' $2 cumulative preferred.

In order to determine this warrant's intrinsic value investors had to multiply the market prices of the three different securities called by the appropriate factor. This was a laborious job, and for this reason alone the Hilton warrant was usually undervalued. Investors were either afraid of it because of its relatively complex terms or were not interested in going through the arithmetic to check on the value of their investment. Naturally, unless a large number of Hilton warrants were held, the exercise of the warrants resulted in the warrantholder receiving odd lots of TWA securities which, when sold, cost in commissions. For these reasons warrants which call a package of shares sell at a smaller premium than other warrants. In fact, these warrants have been known to sell slightly below intrinsic value. Of course, when the difference between the intrinsic value of the warrant and its market value becomes greater than commissions, arbitrageurs move in to correct the situation. In the case of Hilton, which occasionally sold slightly below intrinsic value, an arbitrageur would simultaneously buy the warrant and sell short the three called securities in the ratios that the warrant terms dictate. Some professional arbitrageurs (employees of brokerage houses) pay little or no commissions, resulting in a slim spread between intrinsic and market values, thus eliminating the individual investor from playing the arbitrage game. In fact, if you see a situation where there appears to be a substantial arbitrage profit, check the terms of the warrant carefully before placing your market orders. Because warrants that call a package of securities are not fully understood or properly valued by the investment community, they usually sell at a small premium.

DILUTION PROTECTION

Dilution has two meanings when it comes to warrants. First, a large number of outstanding warrants (or other convertible securities) in relation to the number of common shares issued and outstanding is interpreted by many as a real threat to earnings per share. This ratio is commonly called potential earnings dilution. The theory suggests that conversion of the warrants and other convertibles would result in a substantial drop in earnings per share. The second dilution consideration is the antidilution provisions provided in the warrant agreement to protect the warrantholder.

The earnings dilution syndrome is an interesting one. There are numerous arguments on both sides. However, the facts and logic suggest that a large number of warrants outstanding and therefore supposedly a large potential dilution are not significant in determining warrant prices. The theory is most readily discredited by the fact that the investor does not discount the same thing twice. Since the price of the common has theoretically fully discounted the possible dilution, the price of the warrant does not. However, there is other evidence to suggest that this is not a real problem. Since firms now report earnings on a number of bases, including on a fully diluted basis, investors have a clear idea of what the potential dilution is and they reflect this in their market action. The real question is what would the effective earnings dilution be if there were a full conversion of all outstanding warrants and other convertibles. Since conversion and exercise prices are above zero, the wholesale conversion could result in substantial sums of money flowing into the firm's treasury. One must assume that the firm would put those monies to work and create assets that would result in earnings or just create earnings (as in a marketing campaign). A rational assumption is that these new monies would be put to work as efficiently as other capital recently invested by the firm. The extension of this idea is that, assuming a judicious investment of the monies is made, the potential dilution should be offset by the larger net profit.

Over the past decade a high potential earnings dilution has not had a dampening effect on the warrant price. On the contrary, highly leveraged companies (large debt-to-equity ratio) that made extensive use of convertible debt and warrants often exhibited high price-earnings ratios and high warrant premiums.

The second consideration is the effect on the value of a warrant due to possible capital structure changes. Most warrants have provisions to protect the warrantholder in the event of stock splits, stock dividends, mergers, recapitalizations, and the like. However, the extent of the protection afforded varies extensively. As an example, many warrants are protected against stock dividends, but only those dividends in excess of a certain percentage per year, like 5 percent. This means that the issuer can pay stock dividends of up to 5 percent per year over the life of the warrant and make no changes to the warrant's terms (shares called and exercise price). Some warrants are protected with respect to either shares called or the exercise price, but not both. Again the warrantholder suffers a dilution when there are capital structure changes. Unless a warrant is protected both ways, a warrantholder cannot be confident of maintaining his proportionate call on the potential of the issuer. Those warrants with poor antidilution provisions tend to sell at a lower premium than those with full or nearly full protections.

EXCHANGEABLE WARRANTS

Some warrants are convertible into or exchangeable for common stock during their life or upon expiration. Such warrants are quite unique and require an entirely different method of valuation. There are many such long-term warrants now trading, one being the Warner Communications 'C' Preferred which is really a warrant expiring in 1980, another the Commonwealth Edison (CWE) warrant expiring in 1981. The CWE warrant can, in addition to being exercised at $30 per share, be converted into one-third share of common. This can be done at any time, even after the warrant privilege expires.

To see what effect the conversion feature has on the value of the CWE warrant, in Figure 4–3 Curve *A* represents an estimate of the value of CWE's warrant at various prices for the common stock if the warrant did not carry the conversion right. The conversion value line represents one third of the common price which is the minimum price the warrant must trade at because of the conversion right. For stock prices below the $32 or $33 level the conversion feature provides a greater value for the warrant than does the exercise feature. This means that the CWE warrant has less risk than it would without the conversion feature since it cannot sink below the conversion value line as it otherwise could. Since it has less risk, it is worth more.

Looking at Figure 4–3, we see that the maximum increase in value provided by the conversion feature occurs at about the $22 stock price level, where the distance between Curve *A* and the conversion value line is at its maximum. Measure-

FIGURE 4–3
Commonwealth Edison Warrant

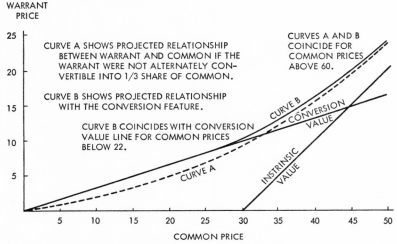

Reprinted with permission of C&P Research, Inc. The above appeared in its June 9, 1971 issue of *C&P Warrant Analysis*.

ment of the spread shows a maximum increase in value of about $1.60. Since at best the conversion feature provides $1.60 worth of added value (or decreased risk), this is the maximum additional premium that investors would want to pay for the warrant. As the level of the stock price increases, the added value of the conversion privilege decreases. It is likely that the added premium would be negligible above the $60 level for the common stock. With this knowledge we can draw Curve *B* which represents an estimate of the value of the Commonwealth convertible warrant at the various stock prices. As shown, this curve merges with the conversion value line below the $22 common level.

The Warner warrant is convertible into only one-sixteenth share of common. This feature becomes significant only at very low stock prices. The Mapco warrant, which expired in

March of 1972, was convertible into one-half share of common only after warrant expiration. During its life this feature often provided a floor for the warrant price.

When warrants such as these are issued they must be evaluated on their individual merits. As a rule, when the stock price is so high as to discount substantially the future utility of the conversion feature, then the warrant acts as rationally as any other. However, at the other end of the spectrum low-risk situations have often developed at reasonable premiums.

NUMBER OF SHARES CALLED

Most warrants are a call on one share of common. As such they are easily evaluated and priced by the public. However, there are many publicly traded warrants which call more than or less than one full share of common. These terms result from mergers, stock splits, and similar events resulting in a change to a warrant's original terms. The Braniff Airways warrant which expires in 1986 currently calls 3.1827 shares of common. Very often warrants that call more than one share are undervalued by the marketplace, almost as if the "secret" were not known. As a result, such warrants are often available at modest premiums.

On the other side are the warrants which call less than a full share. The Mohawk Data Sciences warrant, expiring in 1975, currently calls 0.25 shares; therefore, it takes four warrants to exercise for a full common share. There are many warrants that trade as a call on a fractional share and as a group they are significantly overpriced. In fact, in the last few years the premiums paid for such warrants have been about double the premiums paid for all other warrants. This strongly suggests that most people buying warrants are not fully aware of what they are buying; specifically, they do not know (or are not concerned about) the number of shares called. This has been exemplified most remarkably in a few cases where the called fractional common was available for less than the price of the warrant. In other words, investors were effectively paying more for the warrant than they were for the common which the warrant called, that is, more than the warrant's theoretical maximum value. This is equivalent to paying $10,000 for the option to buy a piece of land which is currently being offered for $9,500! Such situations create some unusual opportunities. Shorting the warrant is one thing that can be done. There are some other trading tactics that are also useful in these cases (see Chapter 7).

There is one way in which you might profit from this market phenomenon wherein fractional warrants are overpriced. If there is a proposed capital structure change in a firm that has a unitary warrant outstanding and that change will result in the warrant's becoming and trading as a fractional warrant, then the situation is worth a close look. Following the greater fool theory it may be possible to profit from this unusual market discrepancy.

SUPPLY AND DEMAND

The overriding factor that determines price in any auction market, such as securities markets, is supply and demand. Very often a temporary oversupply, as in a secondary distribution of a security, will have a deleterious effect on the market price since there is no corresponding jump in demand.

In the field of warrants the *float* is very significant in determining the stability of prices. Some warrants are issued in small quantities (100,000 or less) and trade in a *thin market*, usually OTC. These issues are characterized by large spreads between the bid and asked prices. The bid price often crumbles under the weight of a lot size greater than one hundred warrants. A warrant may be issued in large quantity and still be characterized by a small float. The float is generally considered to be the portion of an issue held in weak hands (public) or available for purchase. A large quantity of warrants may be issued, but it is still possible to have a small float. A large majority of the issuance may be held by insiders and institutions. Since these warrants held in strong hands may not be offered, in spite of possible price movements, the real float can be small. The tip-off is the spread between the bid and asked prices. An illiquid market generally results in a lower price being realized for the warrant. Listed warrants tend to have larger floats, hence more sources of supply and demand. Wall Street has a standard story about the customer who purchased a large number of shares of a low-priced security that traded in a thin market. Much to the customer's satisfaction the issue went straight up in price. When it had doubled in price a few times he called his broker and asked him to sell. The broker replied, "To whom?"

It is very difficult to obtain satisfactory price execution in thin markets. When trading OTC, the quality of the bid and asked prices is always in question when there is a big spread. The large spread is at least indicative of a poor supply-demand marketplace.

UNIMPORTANT FACTORS

There are a couple of significant measures that investors use that one might consider as having an effect on a warrant's price, but they do not. The most important and perhaps the most shocking, are past and current earnings per share. Closely associated with earnings per share is the price-earnings ratio (P/E), and for our purpose here they can be considered one and the same. Warrant investors do not consider current or recent earnings when setting warrant prices. There is a major correlation between warrant and stock prices, but not so much of a correlation between warrant prices and earnings, or *P/E*. There are two reasons for this. First, the optioned stock price is very responsive to earnings, as a rule, and the warrant is very responsive to moves in the optioned stock price. What this suggests is that, once again, warrant investors do not discount the same thing twice. Second, a warrant investor's horizon is usually quite limited—he does not look backward, and his forward vision is within a six-month to three-year range, tending to the shorter side. Warrant investors are not concerned about past or current earnings, therefore, but rather about the immediate and near-term prospects for the underlying stock. These prospects are related to the expectations of Wall Street as to the next few quarterly reports, rather than to earnings trends and the *P/E*. It is also axiomatic that short-term warrant traders are hoping for a quick change in outlook for the firm, which can be expressed in announcements that create market activity.

Another factor which is not significant in determining warrant prices is the past history of the firm. Years of earnings decay, antitrust problems, general litigation, unfavorable government rulings, and other questionable situations do not influence current warrant prices. Warrant investors wipe the slate clean and look ahead. Even when a firm is in deep trouble, warrant investors are willing to pay premiums which are at least equivalent to what is being paid for all other warrants on stable and trouble-free companies.

PRICE LIMITS

A warrant's price is governed by the numerous factors discussed. However, there are two overriding technical factors that restrict a warrant's price to a known channel or range. Figure 3–5 illustrated this range. Depicted here in Figure 4–4 is the same diagram with some minor additions.

You will recall that it is necessary to adjust the price of the warrant if the warrant is a call on a figure other than one full share of stock. As discussed in Chapter 3, the maximum

FIGURE 4–4
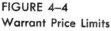
Warrant Price Limits

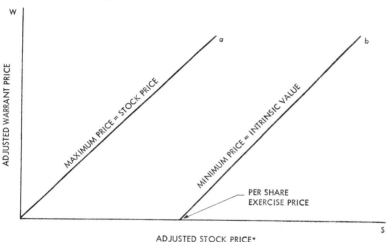

ADJUSTED STOCK PRICE*

* Adjusted prices = actual prices when warrant is a call on one full share and there are no usable bonds.

rational price is the optioned stock price. Who would pay more for an option to buy a piece of land than what the land is currently selling for? Therefore, the maximum price warrant investors are willing to pay for a warrant is the current optioned stock price. This is a good rule of thumb, although occasionally warrants have sold for slightly more than their optioned stock price. The maximum price is illustrated as line *a*, a 45° line emanating from the axis and along which the warrant price equals the stock price. Thus for all possible stock prices the line describes the corresponding maximum warrant price

A warrant's minimum price must be its intrinsic value. If a warrant sold below this price, then arbitrage would tend to correct the aberration. Again, all along line *b* are depicted warrant prices for corresponding stock prices. Point *X* depicts where the minimum price line must start, namely at the exercise price. If the stock sells below the exercise price, then there is no intrinsic value.

NORM PRICE

A warrant's *norm price* is a predicted price, and it is the price at which other warrants with similar characteristics have tended to sell in the past. There is a statistical analysis technique called *multiple regression analysis* which is useful in determining what factors are significant in setting warrant prices. Having identified these factors and assigned real values to them, we are able to predict the current hypothetical worth (norm price) for a given warrant. Suppose we hypothesized that a warrant's price was dependent solely on the underlying stock price and the months to warrant expiration (that is, its remaining life). This can be expressed in a simple arithmetic relationship as follows:

$$W = a + (b)\ (S) + (c)\ (M)$$

where

$$W = \text{warrant price}$$
$$S = \text{stock price}$$
$$M = \text{months to expiration}$$
$$a, b, c = \text{constants.}$$

We could now create a mass of data from historical market and corporate records that relate *W*, *S*, and *M*. In fact, we could come up with thousands of unique sets of data points (W, S, M) by taking daily prices on the stock and warrant for all actively traded warrants. The multiple regression analysis, embodied in a computer program, would relate all of our observations and present us with the values for the constants a, b, and c. It does this by using a least squares step-wise multiple regression technique, which is a fancy way of saying it develops a formula for the curve that depicts a warrant's norm price.[1] Our little equation $W = a + (b)(S) + (c)(M)$ depicts a straight line, which is not really indicative of the real warrant norm price curve but it is sufficient for illustrative purposes. Suppose our multiple regression analysis finds that based upon the historical data points we used that the following form of the equation depicts the norm price:

$$W = .50 + (.3)(S) + (.04)(M)$$

If this were the case, then we could predict the norm price for any warrant using the known values for S and M. As an example, if a warrant were a call for 30 more months on a stock selling at $8, our equation would predict a norm price of:

$$W = \$.50 + (.3)(8.00) + (.04)(30)$$
$$W = \$.50 + 2.40 + 1.20$$
$$W = \$4.10$$

However, there are a number of other factors discussed in this chapter which affect a warrant's price. Using relative stock and warrant prices so that different warrants can be compared, the actual form of the norm price curve is approximated by the equation:

---

[1] For more information about multiple regression analysis see Norman Draper and Harry Smith, *Applied Regression Analysis* (New York: John Wiley & Sons, 1960).

$$\frac{W}{E} = \left[\left(\frac{S}{E}\right)^z + 1\right]^{1/z} - 1$$

where z (which can vary between 1 and infinity), which determines the height and curvature of the warrant curves as shown in Figure 4–5, depends on a host of other factors such that

$$z = a + (b)\ \frac{S}{E}\ + (c)(D) + (d)(V) + \ .\ .\ .\ \text{etc.}$$

Once the multiple regression program has identified which factors (S/E, stock price divided by exercise price; D, dividend; V, volatility etc . . .) are important and has assigned values for the constants ($a,\ b,\ c,\ d,$ etc.), then it is again easy to calculate z, and finally W/E using the cited formula.

In Figure 4–5 a number of different curves are shown for specific values of z.

FIGURE 4–5
Norm Price Curves

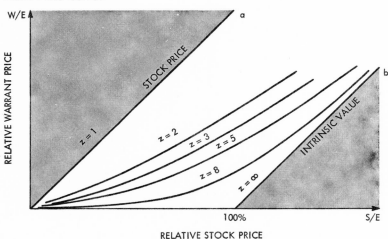

RELATIVE STOCK PRICE

The value of calculating norm prices for currently traded warrants is in identifying over- and underpriced issues. If a warrant has a norm price of $10.00 but sells for $18.50, then it is 85 percent overpriced in relation to what similar warrants have sold for in the past. By the same token, a warrant selling for $7.00 with a norm price of $10.00 is 30 percent underpriced in relation to its norm price. In both cases the issues deserve further attention for possible trading opportunities.

A few norm price equations have been developed over the past 20 years. The usefulness of these numbers is contingent upon the accuracy of the formula developed through multiple regression analysis. The fact that a given warrant is over- or underpriced does not necessarily mean that it will automatically move to its norm price. However, as a class, over- and underpriced warrants do approach their norm price over time. Thus a norm price is a good basis for comparison.

5

The Purchase Decision

THE DECISION TO BUY a warrant is, to the informed, a decision to invest. However, the security is fraught with risks
as well as the possibility of substantial reward. The most
significant part of the evaluation process is the look that you
give the underlying stock, for to purchase a warrant is to
purchase the stock once removed. Spectacular or even good
gains will result from holding a warrant only if the underlying
stock goes up. Fundamental security analysis is the best
known tool for evaluating the prospects for the underlying
stock. If you do not possess these analytical skills, then you
have a long period of study ahead, or you must rely upon the
judgment of reputable analysts. Most investors rely on their
own skills, however limited, and the research reports and
opinions that they can obtain. It is with this in mind that the
techniques recommended herein are presented.

RESEARCH VEHICLES

With the increasing demands for and the improved abilities of publicly owned companies and the investment community to provide volumes of corporate data, this is what is available to the public. If you do not choose to delegate your investment decisions, then you must gather all the available data and, having sifted through it, pick out the significant facts that will lead to an investment decision. There are a number of rather unique avenues of research that should be investigated when you are considering a warrant. First, however, it is important to gather the basic corporate data.

The first thing you must do is determine how much time per week you are willing to spend in your continuing evaluation process. It takes about one half hour per week to keep up with one warrant, based upon the full-blown program outlined below. If you have 10 hours to spare, then you can cover 20 warrants. A list of the 20 warrants you would like to follow avidly should be compiled. Consulting *Moody's Industrial's* or *Standard & Poors' Standard Corporation Records* will provide you with the company address.

It is mandatory that you receive all of a company's reports. The firm will usually add you to its shareholders list, even though you do not own any of its securities. However, your letter will have an added weight if it appears on your letterhead which includes the words "Registered Investment Advisor." It is quite easy and very inexpensive to register with the Securities and Exchange Commission (SEC) as an investment advisor. It is a sad commentary on the law that you need not know a thing about security analysis to qualify. A letter to the SEC in Washington produces the application forms and you are on your way. Armed with your registration and printed letterhead (again, a small expense), you will receive

far better response to your inquiries than you might otherwise. If you want to add some more weight to your punch,
set yourself up under a business name, either a sole proprie-
torship or partnership. The cost to do this in most counties
is negligible. The investment community provides superb
service to a firm registered as an investment advisor.

When writing a company for the first time you should
request a copy of the prospectus that describes the warrants,
a copy of the warrant agreement, and an up-to-date version
of the warrant terms, since these terms may have changed
since the prospectus was issued. Many firms have a public
relations organization that handles many or even all corporate
mailings. Be sure to ask to be placed on the public relations
mailing list as well as the shareholder's list. Through such
organizations as many as two or three "flyers" may be issued
per week, announcing such things as earnings, dividends,
management changes, and significant corporate developments. The object of having such an organization should be
quite obvious; namely, it promotes the stock. Propaganda (in
the form of news releases) is not only sent to you, as an
individual or advisor who has requested it, but to all the
major newspapers, and the numerous analysts and institutions on Wall Street.

Anyone doing his own analysis should read the trade publications on a regular basis. The best are the daily *Wall Street
Journal* and the weekly *Barron's.* Canadian warrants are best
followed by reading *The Financial Post,* a weekly, and *The
Globe and Mail,* the daily business edition. For periodic reference Moody's and Standard & Poor's publish sound material
available in most brokerage offices and public libraries. The
real professional gets part of Standard & Poor's *Standard
Corporation Records,* commonly called the "Daily News."

Published daily, this service reports major corporate news for virtually all companies having actively traded securities. However, the service costs about $250 per year and it takes 15 minutes just to go through it to locate your companies. Standard & Poor's also has a similar *Dividend Record* service.

One of the most significant sources of information is the SEC library, either in New York or Washington. Filing statements, prospectuses, and numerous corporate documents are available. In Washington there is a reprint service, so if you know what you want you can obtain it by writing. The SEC has a lot of information you will not find in an annual report. The SEC also publishes its own, daily *News Digest.* This is very useful in determining what companies have filed a registration statement that includes warrants. There are many reasons, as are discussed later in this chapter, why it is desirable to "be up on a warrant" before it is issued. New registrations are also reported in *Barron's,* but it is far from a complete list. When you become aware of a new registration, write the underwriter asking for the preliminary prospectus, also known as the "red herring."

The major stock exchanges have excellent libraries which are open to the public. For listed warrants you can obtain the application to list, which contains the exact warrant terms as well as a wealth of corporate data. Both the SEC and the exchanges receive periodic reports from companies that as a rule reveal a lot more than annual reports. If you do not have access to any of these key libraries, then the best way to keep informed in detail is to receive all available data from the firm, its public relations outfit or department, and its underwriter, if any. Whenever the firm issues a new prospectus or proxy statement, make sure you get a copy, even though it does not involve new warrants. It will discuss the warrants currently outstanding and also will be chock full of vital information, which is revealed because of the SEC's strict full disclosure rules.

There are a few investment advisory services that specialize in warrants. There are two which are very good. The *C&P Warrant Analysis* (C&P Research, Inc., P.O. Box 123, Ft. George Station, New York, New York 10040) covers all actively traded U.S. and Canadian warrants, well over 400 of them, and provides a wealth of analytical data. This service is most appropriate if you are primarily interested in warrants. *The Value Line Convertible Survey* (Arnold Bernhard & Co., Inc., 5 East 44th Street, New York, New York 10017) covers warrants, convertible preferred stocks, and bonds. This is also a high-quality service, but only covers about 120 warrants, most of which are listed on the major stock exchanges.

As a final note your broker, if large enough, may have a system whereby you can automatically receive all research bulletins on companies you select. The days are gone when you had to buy a share to be kept informed. It is a rare case when a company refuses to send you data it has previously provided to shareholders.

WHAT TO CONSIDER

Only the very unwise investor purchases the common stock of a company without considering the merits of outstanding convertible securities. In fact, it is not uncommon for investors to purchase stock, unaware that there are convertibles in the issuer's capitalization. If one is so sure about the prospects for a firm that a purchase of the stock is justified, then the warrant is usually a much better buy. There may be some added risk that must be considered, but then the potential reward due to the leveraged nature of the security is usually at least offsetting. If less risk is desired, then the investor owes it to himself to consider other convertibles the issuer may have outstanding, such as convertible bonds and preferreds. These securities often provide substantially more downside protection than does the common with little or no lessening of upside potential in relation to the common.

Based on the premise that before purchasing common you will look at the warrant, there are a few critical things you should consider.

First and foremost, you should ascertain when the warrant privilege expires. As a rule, warrants with less than three years of life left should not be purchased. Although you may not intend to hold the warrant for three or even two years, at the two year point the approaching expiration date begins to be a significant factor in systematically reducing the warrant's premium. As a rule, an *expiring warrant* (less than two years of life left) loses value over time even if all other factors (stock price, earnings, earnings prospects, and so forth) remain the same. It takes an exceptional situation to merit holding during these last two years.

All step-ups in exercise price (including the termination of the right to employ a usable bond before warrant expiration) should be carefully evaluated. If the increases in exercise price average 3 percent to 5 percent per year over the remaining life, then it is not usually a great concern. If it is more than 5 percent per year, however, the step-ups may be discounting too much of the hoped for appreciation in the optioned stock. If the average exercise price increase is 10 percent, then this is how much the stock must move per year just to stay even.

The number of shares called can be quite significant in determining warrant prices. As a rule, warrants that call a package of securities tend to sell for less than they are really worth. This is because the terms are not fully understood by the marketplace. More importantly, these warrants do not respond as well as expected to marked increases in one or more of the optioned securities. Based on price histories, there are few examples of where a long position in such a warrant was much more than a waste of time, especially when compared to the performance of even something as broad as an index of warrants. However, a warrant which calls a fractional share of stock is a horse of a different color. These warrants have enjoyed great favor in the marketplace, commanding double the premium awarded other warrants. Again, ignorance of the terms allows these warrants to be priced, more often than not, as if they were a call on a full share. These warrants should not be actively sought for this characteristic alone, but its presence in an otherwise desirable warrant is a definite plus.

When the optioned stock pays a large dividend, then this is foregone by the purchase of the warrant. Although the foregone dividend may not be significant to you, it is to the general public. As a result, warrants which call high-yielding stocks tend to sell for less than otherwise equivalent warrants. For this reason these warrants must have other exceptional characteristics before purchase is justified. Why are the high dividends being paid instead of reinvested? Therefore what are the real appreciation possibilities for the stock, and, as a result, the warrant?

Dilution protection is a most significant factor to consider. The warrantholder should be protected with respect to number *and* kind of shares called as well as the exercise price in the case of stock dividends, stock splits, mergers, combinations, and all recapitalizations. It is also desirable to be protected in the event that the issuer sells stock below the warrant exercise price. If these provisions are not afforded, then great risks are undertaken by the buyer. Do not buy if these protections are not available.

Callable warrants present some unique considerations. There are many warrants that have call provisions. However, only a few warrants have been called in the last 20 years. Nevertheless, in a couple of cases substantial paper and real losses were suffered when warrants with little or no intrinsic value were called at small call prices.

This is not to say that callable warrants should never be considered for purchase if you understand the circumstances which can cause a company to consider calling its warrants. First, remember that not every warrant can be called. The warrant agreement must so provide. Second, there are only a couple of reasons why a firm would invoke the call provision. First, if the company is considering a merger into another company, it may desire to clear the warrants from its capital structure in order to simplify the terms of the merger. This happens rarely but could occur at any time, regardless of the relationship of the common price to the warrant exercise price. Second, the company is in need of cash. A call for this reason will only occur when the common stock price is higher than the warrant exercise price. If this were not true, warrantholders would not exercise and the company would not receive the exercise price. If the common price is too much higher than the exercise price a call would be unlikely since it would be to the company's advantage simply to sell stock on the market rather than force exercise of the warrants. A distinction should also be made between warrants that are callable for a nominal redemption fee (like less than $1.00) and those that provide a fairer compensation to the warrantholder (as does the Bangor Punta warrant, callable at $55).

The following is what is considered to be a reasonable rule

of thumb: Callable warrants should not be ruled out for purchase if the underlying stock is selling for less than half of the exercise price, or is selling for more than one and a half times the exercise price, or if the redemption price is at least one and a half times the current warrant price. Extensive analysis of warrant pricing indicates that investors in general pay little heed to the dangers of callable warrants and in many cases ignore them altogether, paying premiums fully equal to similar premiums paid for warrants that are not callable.

Another major consideration is the quality of the market for the warrant. Since the buyer will wish to sell, he must be assured of a continuing and active market for the warrant. If the warrant is listed on a major exchange, there is no problem. Some over-the-counter warrants trade actively, others do not. A good way to measure the market is to look at two things: the number of warrants outstanding and the nature of the market. If a firm has less than 100,000 warrants outstanding, the chances are that the issue is trading in a thin market. Even though it is fairly actively traded now, the market may deteriorate in the future. Purchase of such warrants is not recommended. The quality of the market is measured by checking the "pink sheets" to determine how many market makers have both bid and asked prices quoted, and what the spread (difference between bid and asked prices) is. Unless there are at least three market makers, the issue is thin. The spread should not be more than 15 percent of the average of the bid and asked prices, or the market is thin. As a rule, you should avoid buying warrants that trade in poor markets as described. It will only make the selling tough. Also, there is a different price depending on which side of the trade you are on. If you are buying you should expect to pay the asked price as a rule. But if you are selling, do not expect to obtain any more than the bid. The difference is the market maker's profit.

WHEN TO BUY

A well-known Wall Street writer, Burton Crane, once said that the best time to purchase the securities of a firm is when "most of the hope is squeezed out." This is the best possible advice. History is full of examples where such a philosophy netted unusual warrant profits. In the years 1942–1946 the R.K.O. warrant went from one sixteenth to $13, enabling an investment of $1,000 to become $208,000. Similarly, $1,000 invested in Tri-Continental grew to $172,000 in just four years. More recently, during 1969–70, the now expired Agau Mines warrant moved from 17 cents to $6.25 in 10 months. This move was a fantastic 3,677 percent, and $1,000 invested on the front end would have yielded $36,765 out the other end a mere ten months later. In all three examples the firms had one thing in common at the low end; there was not an ounce of hope. Things could not have looked worse. This is not to say that all you have to do is buy up all the warrants selling for pennies. This certainly is not the case, and in fact would prove unprofitable if done on a consistent basis. What is significant, however, is that when an established firm is having a temporary (three to five years) rough time, real bargains may develop. Investors should look for established firms in established industries that are currently on the rocks or out of favor. If an issue has dropped at least 50 percent from its high and the firm and/or industry is having its problems, then the situation is worth a close look on the premise that things will not remain that way forever. Sound management will prevail. Following this philosophy the numbers justification is easy. If a security has fallen 50 percent ($90 to $45 as an example), it only has to reach its old high to move up 100 percent. Therefore, genuine turnaround situations are most desirable for the warrant investor.

The single, most crucial consideration requisite to the purchase of a warrant is the evaluation of the optioned stock. The prospects for the firm and its securities must be outstanding to justify purchase. Other than the traditional security analysis considerations (which are beyond the scope of this book) it is desirable that the firm be spending a big chunk of money on research and development. Large sums being reinvested is also a positive sign for warrantholders.

A very positive sign in a warrant is a high ratio of optioned stock price to warrant price, sometimes called the leverage indicator. If the stock sells for $50 and the warrant is at $8, then this value is 6.25, which is considered excellent. This factor becomes important when the stock begins to move up dramatically, hopefully inducing movement in the warrant in at least the same ratio. Although warrants that sell at lower leverage indicator levels (higher warrant price in relation to optioned stock price) can be quite desirable, the ideal warrant will have this leveraged characteristic.

The relation of the current optioned stock price to the exercise price is most important. The ideal warrant calls stock selling at or somewhat below (as much as 40 percent) the exercise price. It is at these levels that there is the most hope that the stock will reach and exceed the exercise price, creating some intrinsic value. This psychological factor creates substantial moves in a warrant's price when the optioned stock moves up within this range. When the common sells at a high multiple of the exercise price the warrant tends to sell at little or no premium. In other words, it sells at its substantial intrinsic value and tends to move in parallel with the stock. As an example, suppose a warrant which calls common at $5 per share sells at $48 while the stock is at $50. Should the stock move to $70, the warrant would probably go to $66. This type of warrant does not provide good leverage and should be avoided. If the stock to exercise price ratio is between 0.6 and 1.3, it is quite acceptable.

Since a long-term gain is generally sought, the warrant should have at least three years of life left.

Potential warrantholders should consider the amount of debt in the capital structure and the firm's philosophy on debt versus equity in fund raising. A high debt-to-equity ratio indicates that the firm is leveraged; that is, it has attempted to raise earnings per share by selling debt as opposed to shares of stock. Assuming that full debt capacity has not been reached, a firm that funds investments with debt as opposed to equity is a friend to the shareholder and warrantholder. If successful, a highly leveraged debt structure results in earnings per share gains that are enviable.

A most important concept in warrant investing is that warrants are bought to be sold, not exercised. Exercising warrants is another way of buying stock. Unless a warrant is purchased at no premium and sells at no premium when exercised, it costs more to buy stock through exercise than it does to do so outright. There are only two exceptions to the rule. First, if a warrant sells significantly below its intrinsic value, arbitrage, which involves purchase and exercise of the warrants along with a short sale of the stock, is justified. Second, the tax laws sometimes force us to do unnatural things. To insure a long-term gain or a short-term loss exercise is occasionally desirable.

The size of the premium to be paid is a major buy consideration. Premium is the price we pay for leverage. The ideal situation is to find a warrant having a small or nonexistent

FIGURE 5–1
Normal Warrant Prices and Premiums*

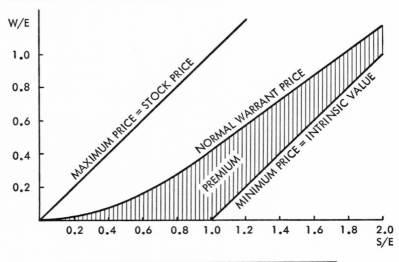

S/E	W/E	Premium	S/E	W/E	Premium
0.10	0.02	920%	1.10	0.48	35%
0.20	0.04	420	1.20	0.53	28
0.30	0.07	256	1.30	0.62	25
0.40	0.09	173	1.40	0.69	21
0.50	0.11	122	1.50	0.75	17
0.60	0.14	90	1.60	0.85	16
0.70	0.21	73	1.70	0.92	13
0.80	0.26	58	1.80	1.02	12
0.90	0.34	49	1.90	1.09	10
1.00	0.42	42	2.00	1.16	8

* For warrants with at least two years of life left.
Adjusted per share prices must be used when using table.

premium while retaining all the other positive characteristics
discussed. This is next to impossible; therefore, the question
arises as to what is a normal or reasonable premium. In terms
of Figure 4–5 the premium is the difference between the
intrinsic value line and the curve that represents the warrant
in question. Using one normal warrant price curve, which is

the average of all those shown in Figure 4–5, we have the results shown in Figure 5–1. This depicts the typical or average warrant.

As you will recall, the premium is the difference between the warrant price (adjusted) and its intrinsic value (which can be negative) expressed as a percentage of the stock price. The area between the normal warrant price curve and intrinsic value line represents the positive premiums paid for the average or "normal" warrant. Of course, when the stock sells below the exercise price (S/E less than 1.0) all of the warrant price is premium; and the premium may be substantially more than 100 percent when the warrant sells with negative intrinsic value. As is evident, when the stock price is a multiple of the exercise price (S/E is greater than 1.0), the premium is small. This is reflected in the diagram as the normal warrant curve approaches the intrinsic value line. At the low end (S/E less than 1.0) premiums become progressively larger until at the very low end they are astronomical. When $S/E = 0.10$, as an example, the stock must go up 10 times just to reach an intrinsic value on the warrant of zero. The table represents typical or normal premiums for warrants that have at least two years of remaining life. When the stock sells at the exercise price, a 42 percent premium is not unreasonable. Since it is desirable to purchase warrants when S/E ranges between 0.6 and 1.3, a range of reasonable premiums is 25 percent to 90 percent, as shown in Figure 5–1. One way of rationalizing the premium paid is to consider that the difference between the stock price and the warrant price is a hypothetical loan. You are putting up less money than the purchaser of common, yet you control the same quantity of stock. The common purchaser might put up less than the full purchase price by buying on margin. The margin trader pays interest on the amount borrowed. The warrant premium can be considered equivalent to these interest payments. Of course, the real reason for premiums is the warrant's inherent leverage that must be paid for. As a rule of thumb, it takes an exceptional situation to justify purchase of a warrant that requires paying more than a 90 percent premium.

By now it should be evident that the higher the leverage indicator, the better the prospects for the speculator. An indicator of 2.0 is the minimum acceptable level, 2.5 to 4.0 is a good range, and anything above 4.0 is excellent leverage. As would be expected, expiring warrants (especially during the last few months) generally exhibit fantastic leverage. However, the purchaser is betting that this leverage will be achieved in a very short period of time.

Another useful measure of a warrant's worth as a buy is the deviation from its normal price. By comparing it to what other warrants with similar characteristics have sold for in the past, we can determine whether the issue is over or underpriced. If it is significantly underpriced, then it is worth a closer look. Figure 5–1 is most useful in helping you to do this. All that is required is that you calculate S/E and W/E, plot it on the chart, and see if the point is significantly below the normal warrant price curve. As an example, suppose you are considering a warrant which calls one share of common at $15 for three more years. The stock sells at $20, and the warrant is at $7. Since the warrant calls one full share, as opposed to a fractional share or a package, and there is no usable bond, there is no need to adjust the warrant and exercise prices. If there are such conditions when you test other warrants, be sure to adjust the prices so they are representative of a call on one full share. In our example S/E is $20 divided by $15 which is 1.33 and W/E is $7 divided by $15 which is 0.47. Using a pencil point as a guide on Figure 5–1, you can see that the point where $S/E = 1.33$ and $W/E = 0.47$ is well below the normal price curve. This suggests that the warrant may be undervalued. Similarly, using the table in the same figure 5–1, it is possible to calculate the premium associated with this point on the graph and compare it to the actual premium being paid in the marketplace. The calculated W/E was 0.47. This lies between 0.42 and 0.48 in the W/E column of the table, so the normal premium lies between the indicated 35 percent and 42 percent. By simple interpolation we can arrive at the exact figure. The difference between the W/Es is 0.06 (0.48 minus 0.42). The difference between the premiums is 7 percent (42 percent minus 35 percent). The W/E we are interested in is 0.01 away from 0.48 and represents one sixth of the difference between the two table entries. Therefore, if we take one sixth of the 7 percent and add it to the 35 percent, we will move up an amount of premium equivalent to the one sixth movement in W/E. Therefore the interpolated premium is 36.2 percent (35 percent + 7 percent/6). This is the normal premium. Based on the known prices we can calculate the actual premium as 10 percent ($7 less $5 all divided by $20). It should be evident that this technique is most useful in evaluating new issues, especially if the terms are known before trading begins. When evaluating a warrant using these methods it is important that the warrant have at least two years of remaining life. If it does not, then you must adjust the calculated W/E or premium appropriately. This is done by a prorating of the W/E value or premium amount over the remaining months. If the predicted W/E is 0.45 and months to expiration are 20, then you should adjust the W/E to 0.38 (0.45 times 20/24). Similarly, if the warrant has only one month to go before expiration, its adjusted W/E would be 0.02 (0.45 times 1/24). This technique accounts for the premium loss that a warrant experiences as it approaches expiration.

To summarize, the ideal warrant for purchase is one which has the following 10 basic characteristics:

1. Call on stock selling close to the exercise price.
2. High leverage indicator.
3. Low premium (20 percent or less) and cheap in relation to norm price.
4. Long call (three or more years).
5. Full dilution protection.
6. No scheduled terms changes, such as exercise price step-ups.
7. Active market.
8. Little or no dividend on optioned stock.
9. Not callable.
10. Sound prospects for underlying stock.

One Wall Street saw suggests that we should put all our eggs in one basket, then watch that basket very carefully. The antithesis of this is complete diversification, as in a broad-based mutual fund. Since warrants impose certain risks, they also carry certain individual investor responsibilities. One such responsibility is conservative diversification. If a portfolio is to have a long position in warrants, it should be spread among at least five different issues.

WHEN TO SELL

The only rational time to sell is when objectives have been met, on the up *or* downside. On the date of purchase objectives should be set to include the downside tolerance point (stop loss) where a sell is used to end an unfortunate investment. The upside objective should be both price and date oriented. To hang on to a mediocre position in the hopes that it will work out is to incur a significant opportunity cost (loss). Your money would probably be more productive in another position. There is an adage on Wall Street that you should cut your losses short, but let your profits run. This makes sense and should be used to temper your upside objectives. If on the target date, or before, your performance objective has been met and the warrant is still going straight up, then maybe a new date and new profit objective is in order, theoretically considering that you simultaneously closed and reopened the position. Strict personal discipline is a must for successful investing, in warrants or anything else.

One rule of thumb which has been used in the past is that a sale of all long positions is in order when warrants as a group reach 40 percent of their optioned stock prices. This is akin to saying the market is a buy when the *P/E* on the Dow is below 15 to 1, and it is a sell at 21 to 1 and over. However, a more significant measure is the premium. If a warrant is purchased at a reasonable premium, then the time to sell on the upside is when the premium becomes unreasonable, that is, when the warrant becomes overpriced. By the same token, if a warrant is purchased when it is selling significantly below its normal price and then it comes into line, it is usually a sign to sell.

When warrants are issued in units with other securities, the tax laws sometimes influence the decision to sell. Suppose a unit is sold for $20, consisting of a share of stock and one warrant. The warrant begins trading OTC at $2.50. Under the current tax laws you, as the purchaser, have a choice for establishing a cost base. You may value the warrant at zero, in which case the share of stock has a cost basis of $20. Upon sale of the warrant a gain equal to the sale price must be reported. However, if you wish to allocate the $2.50 to the warrant as its cost basis, then you assign $17.50 to the stock. On the premise that you wish to retain the warrant and sell off the stock, it is possible to establish a $2.50 cost basis for the warrant and possibly sell the stock on the day of issuance at a short-term loss. Upon the sale of the warrant you will realize a capital gain or loss, depending on whether you receive more or less than the amount of cost basis which you have allocated to the warrant. If the warrant is to be sold while the shares are to be kept, then it may be advisable to sell on opening day, take the warrant price as the cost basis so there is no gain, and hold the stock at the lower of two possible cost bases.

BUYING NEW ISSUES

At the present time there are about two new warrants issued per week. Some of these are issued by firms going public; others are issued by established firms which already have publicly traded securities. With very few exceptions new warrants are issued in units with some other security, such as stock or bonds. In raging bull markets, which characterized a number of periods during the 1960s, choosing the right new issue was relatively easy. They all went up, trading higher than the issue price on the day of offering. The only problem was getting your hands on enough of a new issue to make it worthwhile. Brokers rationed their allotments of new stock, favoring their better customers. Unless you generated significant commission income for your broker, there was little chance to participate for more than a few shares or units. Even in bear markets the new issues that are able to make it to market tend to sell out quite quickly, although they do not all immediately go to a substantial premium. In bull or bear markets it is worth the trouble to keep track of and participate occasionally in new issues. If a desirable warrant can be obtained at the issue price from your broker, that is just fine. However, chances are that you will be able to obtain the warrant in the *after market*, public trading as in any other security, at little or no real additional cost.

Due to the warrant's unique nature and the fact that it is often issued in units, unusual values occasionally develop upon issuance. This undervaluing of the warrant may continue for the first few days or even weeks of trading. First, consider the unique nature of the warrant. The security is not fully understood by the general investing public. Hence, when warrants are issued in a unit, as with a share of stock, many of those who subscribe to the new issue immediately sell off the unwanted component, namely the warrant. There are also some institutions, like pension funds, which by charter are prohibited from owning warrants or other options but wish to subscribe to the bond or stock through the exercise of rights. Between the unknowing public and the restricted institutions a large supply of warrants may hit the market during the few weeks following the offering. Such activity depresses the warrant price and often creates bargains for the knowledgeable. When A.T.&T. issued warrants in 1970 it found that a massive educational program (written material and public information centers) was required to answer the thousands of inquiries from shareholders who had received rights to subscribe to units of debt and warrants. Of course, the inquiries were related to the nature of the attached warrants. Once in a while the public is given a bonus by an unknowledgeable or cagey underwriter who underprices the units, thus placing an unrealistically low value on the warrants. The price of any public issue is a negotiated one. The issuer wants to obtain the highest possible price for the securities. In the interests of selling the issue quickly and providing its customers with an assured capital gain, the underwriter argues for a low price. When the issuer loses, the public wins. Since few issuers are capable of assigning a premarket value to the convertible component of a unit, they are at the mercy of their trusted underwriters, or must employ the services of an outside consultant. As a rule, they figure the warrant as part of the cost of the underwriting and therefore do not consider its true value. As a result of the unusual circumstances that surround the issuance of warrants, avid warrant investors should be prepared to take advantage of the unusual opportunities that occasionally develop. Speed is of the essence, for the undervaluing may be only momentary, lasting up to a few weeks at most. A lot of preissuance spade work must be done.

The first indication that a new warrant is in the wings comes when the issuer files a registration statement with the SEC. This may lead to an issue within a month, but more commonly the lead time is three to ten months. The registration for *all* new warrants is reported in the *SEC News Digest*, while most are reported in the Daily News Section of Standard & Poor's *Standard Corporation Records* and the major ones are reported in the major trade publications, such as *Barron's* and *The Wall Street Journal.* Canadian registrations are reported in *The Financial Post.* A few weeks after registration, a preliminary prospectus, called the *red herring,* is available. This should be obtained, for it contains the majority of information that will constitute the basis for the investment decision. Those who are able to get to a SEC library have the added advantage of more information than is usually contained in the preliminary prospectus.

When you have gathered all the required data, it is necessary for you to determine a fair value for the warrant before issue. Your best method of doing this is to select a range of probable exercise prices (unless one has been specified prior to issue, which is quite unusual). Most warrants are issued with an exercise price which is 10 percent to 25 percent above the optioned stock price upon the day of issue. As you conjecture upon where the stock will be upon issue, you can develop a range of stock prices, and for each stock price a corresponding range of probable exercise prices. Since you lack a sophisticated normal price equation which would help predict the expected value, you must assign what you feel are fair values for the warrant in each stock-exercise price combination you have come up with. If a usable bond is to be considered, then the job is more complicated but not impossible. If the coupon rate is known, then a market bond price can be estimated by finding an equivalent security in the issuer's capitalization, or, lacking that, in the industry. If the issuer's bond is rated by Moody's or Standard & Poor's, then all you have to do is find another bond in the same industry with a similar coupon and rating. Armed with these data, you can calculate an adjusted per share exercise price. Fair warrant values are arrived at by calculating hypothetical prices based on assumed leverage and premium figures. Figure 5–1 may be useful in determining the appropriate normal price and premium that should be paid. If the issue comes out at or trades substantially below your calculated price, then it may be a bargain. Beware of warrants that call high-interest-paying securities, such as shares of beneficial interest issued by Real Estate Investment Trusts. This type of warrant has traditionally sold at a modest premium in spite of good leverage.

BUY-SELL GUIDELINES

Before investing or speculating in warrants, you should establish your own personal rules of the road. These rules should be very personal, reflecting the amount of risk you are willing to take for an expected reward. Your investment philosophy should be an extension of your personality. Do not try to emulate one person (Bernard Baruch, for example) in the marketplace, another in your personal life, and another in business life. In order to invest rationally you must establish a firm set of guidelines. Most investors who continually lose money in the market, and there are many, can attribute several losses to their emotional reaction to current conditions. If all investors were completely rational when making investment decisions, the volatility of the market as a whole and of individual issues would be substantially reduced. It does not hurt to write down your own guidelines, referring to them when the going is rough. Some of the ones presented here have proved useful to many investors. The list becomes meaningful only when augmented and tempered by personality and experience.

One basic rule which is often violated is to buy only when the fundamentals of the common are good. Associated with this is the notion of risk and diversification. If you disregard risk, there is no need to diversify, for there is one warrant that will outperform all others over a given period of time. The most profitable speculation, then, is to place all funds in one security, the one that is to perform better than all others. Finding this issue is the only obstacle. Because the preceding is almost impossible and highly fraught with risk, investors diversify. By spreading assets across industries and firms the individual reduces the impact of a mistake. Selecting warrants with good underlying fundamentals also tends to reduce the risk.

Before making a commitment you should set objectives, especially on the downside. If the position does not act as expected, get out. Holding a sliding warrant and entering the "locked-in syndrome" is a significant mistake. Not only are you losing money on the depressed issue, but you incur an opportunity cost, that is, the amount that the locked-in money might be generating in another position. Selling, if objectives are not met (even at a loss), is always preferable to being locked in, hoping for a miracle.

Very often investors follow the "crowd." The crowd is a consensus that reflects tips, rumors, politics, security analysts' opinions, and personal optimism or pessimism. Wall Street is a hotbed of emotion, the impact of which is constantly increasing due to advances in communications. To be swayed by the crowd is to become irrational about your market decisions.

Buying on weakness and selling on strength, either market, industry or corporate, is a well accepted philosophy. Taking a long rather than a short-term view is also desirable. Short-term traders are, on the whole, losers. Do not buck the market. The majority of small investors tend to do this, as evidenced by the odd-lot trading statistics. The small investor tends to be a "one eighth man"; that is, he places orders to squeeze out the most profit or to minimize the loss. The risk of not having the order executed and the warrant go down far outweighs the increment of the one eighth or one fourth. By the same token, do not be commission-conscious. Market objectives should preclude the impact of commissions. Placing market orders for listed issues is a good policy to follow.

In addition to considering the fundamentals, the technical position of the warrant should be evaluated. Such things as supply, demand, short position (available only if listed), and price history are relevant.

Before buying the common of any concern, find out if there is a warrant available. Before purchasing the warrant, investigate the possibilities of a hedge position. A hedge position tends to reduce the risk of loss, as well as reducing the magnitude of possible gain. Most investors value the reduction in risk more highly than the associated limitation on gain.

6

Some Profitable
Trading Techniques
for Warrants

S INCE WARRANTS can be either overvalued or undervalued
by the marketplace, there are some trading techniques
especially designed to take advantage of such situations.

SHORT SELLING

Short selling is a trading technique you use when you feel
that the security being sold will go down in price. When you
sell something short, you do not own it. The securities you
sell are loaned to you by someone who owns or holds them.
You *cover* your short position when at a later date you buy
the securities, hopefully at a lower price. The securities
bought are returned to the lender, either an individual or a
broker. If your evaluation is correct, you will be able to buy
at a lower price the securities that you previously sold short,
thus creating a profit.

Short selling has always been thought of as a bold tactic, since unlike a long position there is supposedly unlimited risk. When you buy a warrant, the lowest it can go is to zero. However, you might sell short at (let us say) $10, then watch the security rise to $100, $1,000, or even higher. Assuming you do not cover at a loss somewhere on the way up, your risk exposure is almost infinite. This basic fact of short selling has kept many investors away from the short side of the market. However, markets and individual securities rise and fall over time, and it would seem that if short selling is not part of an investor's repertoire, then he is missing half of the opportunities.

Many people believe that short selling is risky because short sellers in any security constitute a future demand for that security. The reasoning suggests that the larger the short position in any security, the larger the potential demand. Most short sellers limit their upside risk by putting in a *stop loss order*. This is a directive to a broker to act at a specified price. Therefore, if you sell short at $10, you might place a stop loss limit order at $12.50, limiting your loss (without consideration of margin and commissions) to 25 percent. This is a standing order as a rule, *good until cancelled* as it is called in the trade, which will be lined up with all the other stop loss orders on the *specialist's book*. This is a list of open orders kept by the specialist at the *trading post* on the exchange floor where the market is made in your security. The specialist is responsible for making a market in a number of securities. He may have a number of other orders at $12.50, in which case yours would not be executed until all others entered before yours had been. If the market should *sell through* your limit of $12.50, before your order could be executed, then by exchange rules your order becomes a *market order*, that is, it no longer has a limit price of $12.50 but will be bought at the best price. It is possible that you might be bought in for somewhat more than $12.50 in a fast moving market. However, this happens only about 15 percent of the time and when it does the difference is almost always less than a point. One of the specialist's duties is to maintain an orderly market in his securities. To do this he must often trade against the market for his own account. In the example of a runaway security on the upside the specialist, by exchange bylaw, must be in there selling (either long or short) to help stabilize the situation. Thus the use of stop loss orders, in either direction, is strongly recommended to limit losses. In the case of the short seller the use of the stop loss is an effective way to limit upside risk. There is also some fiction to the notion that a heavy short position in a security (10 to 20 percent of the outstanding shares or warrants) is creating a dangerous, future demand condition. Recall that when you sell short you must borrow the securities sold. When you sell them to someone, it is said that you represent a future demand for the securities. However, the person to whom you sold them now represents a future supply. The balance between future supply and demand has not changed, only the magnitude of it has changed! In brief, selling short creates supply as well as demand. Let us take a simple, unrealistic, but illustrative example. A firm has 100,000 warrants outstanding. The register of warrantholders looks like this:

Holder	Warrants Owned
James	40,000
Jones	25,000
Smith	10,000
Thompson	25,000

You feel that a short in the warrants would be appropriate, so you direct your broker to sell short 10,000 warrants at the market. To do this your broker borrows 10,000 warrants from James, who is willing and able to lend them to you. Your broker also finds a buyer, Williams. Now the register looks like this:

Holder	Warrants Owned
James	40,000
Jones	25,000
Smith	10,000
Thompson	25,000
Williams	10,000

The supply just went up 10 percent. This adequately offsets your future demand. You are a potential buyer, Williams a potential seller. James still owns 40,000 warrants. He only *loaned* the 10,000 to you. At his option he can sell his 40,000 warrants, 10,000 of which your broker immediately borrows from someone else. In large, listed issues this is usually very easy. Thus, a 25 percent short position in a security implies that there are people holding borrowed stock who think they own it (they actually do for all intents and purposes). The extent of their ownership is exactly 25 percent of the outstanding issue, completely offsetting the potential demand. Another phenomenon of the short sale is that in the case of a dividend's being paid on the security, there may be more than one account vying for the same dividend payment, since more than one account can "own" the security. To meet this potential problem the rules require that the borrower of securities pay the dividend to the lender. In our example, assuming that the security was stock instead of a warrant, you as the borrower would be obligated to reimburse James for all dividends paid on his stock. Williams, or more appropriately his brokerage house, as holder of record would receive the payment from the company. Therefore, if you are short a dividend paying security, be prepared to absorb the payments as part of the cost of carrying the position. It is also interesting to note that the net effect of this dividend situation is that more dividends are actually paid and reported as taxable income than are declared and paid by the company. If the short position in a security is 25 percent, then the real dividend payment (exchange of funds) is 25 percent more than it would be if there were no short position and only the company was making payments.

BORROWING FOR SHORT SALES

Short selling requires that your broker borrow the securities to be sold short. In some cases this is quite easy (they may be right in his own house); at other times it is quite difficult or next to impossible.

Many houses have rules that restrict short selling to certain securities. Some require that the security sold short be *marginable;* other houses also fix a price (like $3.00) below which they will not sell securities short. Marginable securities are those listed on an exchange and the OTC securities which appear on the Federal Reserve System's (FED) approved list. This is a limited list of actively traded OTC securities with large floats. In the recent past the list has not included warrants. However, the major exchanges provide thousands of stocks and hundreds of warrants which are marginable and therefore represent a potential supply for short sellers.

When an investor buys an issue on margin, he must sign an agreement with his brokerage house which includes a provision allowing the house to lend the purchased shares to another investor for short selling. This is why marginable securities are relatively easy to short and why some houses limit short sales to these securities. Note, however, that the house may lend you shares it holds in its own account or shares owned by another client (if it can obtain permission to do so) even if the securities are not marginable. Even if the securities are not available in-house, they can be borrowed from another brokerage house that has an available supply.

The natural question to ask now is: "What if the lender wants his securities back? Am I bought in, possibly at a great loss?" Once you have sold short you are obligated to return the securities upon request. From a practical point of view, however, this is not significant and you as the individual investor are not aware that this is happening. If the lender wishes to sell what he has lent to you, more than likely his broker will have other securities he can use for the transaction. If not, your broker will attempt to borrow from another broker. Finally, some brokerage houses will temporarily fail to deliver the issue and actually have a net short position in the security. Those who short listed securities are seldom bought in. There are cases where people (supposedly professionals) have been bought in after shorting unmarginable securities, which suggests that it is unwise to short unmarginable securities; that is, those OTC issues not on the FED's approved list. This is also quite difficult to do. Your broker must find someone who owns the OTC security and is willing to lend it. Since it cannot be margined, it must be found in someone's *cash account* (types of accounts include cash, margin, bond, short) or in his own name at home. This is not easy to do.

One other potential obstacle to short selling is a broker's ignorance of the laws and procedures for same, or plain laziness. Some brokers just will not look (call other houses) for securities you wish to short. Others will search out all avenues. If your current brokerage house is of the former nature, get a new one.

SHORT SELLING AS A TRADING TACTIC

Short selling requires a prior conviction that the issue is drastically overpriced, or that the market is going to plunge, dragging good and bad with it. Since profits arising from short sales are taxed as short-term capital gains, no matter how long the position is held, your prognosis should be that a dip is imminent. Shorting overvalued warrants can be profitable; but, due to the highly leveraged nature of the security, it is fraught with risk. Occasionally a warrant violates the rules of the game and actually trades for more than the security it calls. This happened in 1971 with the Ling-Temco-Vought "Okonite" warrant and provided a splendid short selling opportunity. For those who wish to limit the risk there are two courses of action. First, the stop loss order can be employed. Second, the short position can be *hedged* by other securities of the issuer.

Short selling over the years has provided some spectacular profits for the iron-willed. Wall Street suggests that the tactic is not for the fainthearted, and this is good advice. The use of stop loss orders as a modus operandi limits the potential because the short seller (assuming the stop is something like 20 percent above the short sale price) will be stopped out enough on the upside to eat up most of the profit made on the downside. A true short seller has the resources (cash or marginable securities to meet margin requirements) and the intestinal fortitude to wait out a rise in a shorted issue in anticipation of the fall. Strength of conviction is a must. There is a story about one man who exhibited the ultimate in this area. In the late 1920s RCA was the glamour stock. It was to the 1920s what IBM was to the 1960s. As prices rose it became extremely overvalued and sold at huge *P/E*s, more than 100 to 1. This man began going short at about $150. When the stock reached $200 his friends suggested he cover. His reply was to short more, reasoning that if he was right at $150, he was that much more right at $200. The stock rose to $230, $250, and $280, and he shorted it all the way up, using vast resources and an iron will as his guide. Meanwhile his friends chastised him. When RCA broke $300 he shorted more! When he covered at $5 per share in 1930, who was right? Of course, the break of 1929 helped, but it was because of the overvalued RCAs of the time that we had the break, not vice versa. Most investors do not have the resources and willpower to effect a series of successful short sales. This trading tactic, barring special knowledge of the situation, is best left to the professionals. However, there are hedging techniques, as discussed below, which employ short selling and are appropriate for all profit-minded investors.

THE WARRANT HEDGE

Whenever you feel strongly about the prospects for a given warrant but do not wish to incur the full risk of a straight buy, then a warrant hedge is in order. In addition to buying the undervalued warrant, you short the optioned stock in a ratio to the warrants long that attempts to maximize the *risk-reward matrix*. This matrix is nothing but a tabular or graphic illustration of the risks and rewards inherent in the position. The ideal warrant hedge is one wherein the risk-reward matrix is such that we do not care which way the warrant moves; that is, we expect to profit on either side. This is an unusual situation, but it has happened!

Warrant hedges are most useful when a warrant appears to be technically undervalued. In this situation we purchase the warrant, hoping that it will become more appropriately valued in relation to the optioned stock. If we were "supremely confident" that the stock was poised on the launching pad (that is, we possess some unique or undisclosed information), there would be no need to hedge the position. A straight buy would be more appropriate. Since warrants are leveraged, we expect an undervalued warrant to advance much more rapidly percentagewise than the optioned stock. As a result, a short position in the stock equal in dollar amount to the long warrant position tends to reduce the upside potential (but not eliminate it) while limiting the downside risk.

WARRANT HEDGE INVESTMENT

Current Federal Reserve Board (FRB) regulations make warrant hedges even more exciting and potentially profitable. FRB *Regulation T* stipulates that an investor can sell securities short *without putting up any money* to support the short position provided that other securities convertible within 90 days into the shorted securities are held in his account. "Reg T," as it is called, has profound implications for the warrant investor. Warrants do indeed qualify as convertible securities under the law even though money must be put up (the exercise price) only when converting. Buying a warrant is not unlike purchasing the convertible but not the principal component of a convertible bond. Since the price of the warrant does not include the loan segment, it is much cheaper than the equivalent in bonds and therefore increases the warrant investor's leverage substantially. Let us take an example: A firm has a warrant outstanding which calls common at $20 per share for five years. The stock is at $20 and the warrant is undervalued at $4. There is also a convertible bond outstanding which is convertible into 40 shares of common stock. At a minimum this bond is worth $800 (40 shares times $20), but may sell at $1,000 because it pays interest and, like a warrant, enjoys a premium. To an investor the bond coupon rate may be set at $70 while the conversion privilege is worth $800. Now, to offset a short position of 200 shares, five bonds must be held with a value of $5,000. However, the same short position can be offset by holding 200 warrants, requiring an investment of only $800. Herein lies the leverage of using warrants in conjunction with Reg T. Since profits must be measured in terms of the investment made, the warrant hedge by definition just has to be more favorable than a convertible bond hedge. Of course there is more risk, since the coupon paid on bonds tends to put a floor on the bond price. However, the increased profitability of the warrant hedge more than offsets the added risk.

A real-life example is the best way to illustrate how the warrant hedge works. Ling-Temco-Vought (LTV), the proud backer of a number of warrants, had an OTC warrant which expired on January 10, 1972 and which in the Spring of 1970 called 1.0056 shares of common at $49.72 per share. Since LTV had a number of other listed warrants, this one drew less attention from investors. As a result, it was very often found to be underpriced. In the early 1960s LTV was a "swinging" conglomerate. However, by the turn of the decade the outlook for the debt-burdened outfit was bleak. Since the warrant exercise price ($49.72) was substantially above the stock price (1970–71 range was 29⅛ to 7⅛) during 1970–72, the warrant tended to sell at a small fraction of the stock price. This ingredient is important, as will become evident. Also significant is that when LTV common drifted down, the warrant tended to become more undervalued, and when it jumped up it moved more into line with the normal, expected price. At the low end the downside risk was minimal (the warrant just could not go much lower no matter what happened to the stock). On the upside the stock was quite volatile, spurting when the market rose. Here was an ideal warrant hedge candidate, which possessed the three critical characteristics: (1) undervalued warrant presenting minimal downward risk; (2) volatile common; and (3) a high ratio of stock price to adjusted (call one share) warrant price.

On May 1, 1970 the LTV '72 warrant traded at $1.25 while the stock stood at $16.13. At that point the warrant appeared to be worth more like $3.75, based on either a norm price evaluation or a schedule of premium ratios. (See Figure 5–1.) At the time it was appropriate to enter into at least a "two to one" hedge; that is, to sell one common share short for two warrants purchased. Suppose you entered into the following position:

```
200 LTV '72 warrants long ....................... $250.00
100 LTV common short.........................        ...
                                                ─────────
    Investment................................  $250.00
```

Normally you would have to put up as much as $1,613.00 in order to support the short position (less if margin requirements are utilized). However, under Reg T the $250.00 investment in the warrants is sufficient. In fact, since each warrant called 1.0056 shares of stock, in large volume the warrants would support more than the 200 common shares short that they would under the usual conditions where a warrant calls one share. Therefore, in the above example we have used only slightly less than half of the "shorting power" that the warrants provide. The real kicker here is that for a mere $250 you could have controlled as much as a $3,226.00 short position! On this full support basis a minor drop in the stock without a drastic drop in the warrants results in a profit! Now let us see what happened to the more conservative LTV '72 two-to-one hedge. Although there were some intermediate points where you could have jumped off, playing by the rules which suggest that you wait for the warrant to become more fairly valued in relation to the stock, the position should have been closed a few weeks later on May 29, 1970. At that time the stock had fallen from $16.13 to $9.88, but the warrant, undervalued to start with, fell to only 75 cents. The hedge worked as expected on the downside. The results were great:

Loss on 200 warrants long	$(100.00)
Gain on 100 common short	625.00
Net gain	$ 525.00

This gain of $525.00 represents an actual gain of 210 percent on the investment of $250. However, on an annualized basis the position was open for 28 days, yielding a very respectable 2,738 percent (210 times 365/28)! This is not just conjecture and hindsight. At this time this intelligent hedge was recommended by and entered into by a number of knowledgeable investors.

Although there is no method of predicting when you may have gotten out if you missed the early boat, we can conjecture about what would have happened if LTV common went the other way; and in fact, later in the year it did just that. On October 2, 1970 LTV common had risen to $16.75 with the warrant moving more into line at $2.13. At this point the position, if still open, should have been closed with the following results:

Loss on 100 common short	$ (62.00)
Gain on 200 warrants long	176.00
Net gain	$114.00

Although not as nice as the gain in the other direction, there was still a gain. Another hedge position could have been entered here on March 2, 1971 when the LTV '72 warrant sold down to 50 cents when the stock was at $15.00. Even though the warrant was due to expire in less than a year, the risk-reward matrix just looked too good. The ratio might have been more appropriate at four- or five-to-one at this point. On May 21, 1971 the warrant had gone up to $2.75 on a move to $18.13 on the common. At the four-to-one ratio the score would have looked like this:

Loss on 100 common short	$(313.00)
Gain on 400 warrants long	900.00
Net gain	$ 587.00

On an annualized basis this was a gain of 1,339 percent on the $200.00 invested in the warrants. Over its life this warrant provided numerous other opportunities for hedging profits. It always reacted as predicted and was very nice to its friends.

Other low-priced and at the same time undervalued warrants have presented similar opportunities. The same kind of numbers can be generated by looking at the history of the General Host and Chris-Craft warrant-stock prices. Of course the three key questions are:

1. How do you identify the opportunity?
2. What is the appropriate ratio?
3. When do you get out?

IDENTIFYING WARRANT HEDGE OPPORTUNITIES

A warrant hedge position is most useful in exploiting a warrant that is technically undervalued. If you believe that a warrant is fundamentally undervalued (that is, the underlying stock itself is a good buy), then there is no need to hedge your warrant buy. Very often, due to a temporary imbalance of supply and demand as a result of a short-range condition (in the market or the issue), warrants sell significantly below their true value. This aberration in price is usually short-lived, suggesting that one must act quickly. This fact often prevents the investor from performing a thorough, fundamental analysis of the underlying stock. Thus a warrant hedge is usually a bet that the warrant and stock will move into line, more than it is a bet on which way the stock will go. In fact, in entering a warrant hedge, an investor would be delighted if the warrant rose and the stock fell (it has happened!), but he is quite satisfied if his judgment on the technical value of the warrant is correct and it goes up while the stock remains stationary. He is also pleased if the stock falls out of bed and the warrant finds its floor at a point that provides a good profit. Therefore, a warrant hedge is also useful in limiting the risk in what otherwise might have been a straight short in the stock. If you are completely sure about the downfall of a stock, there is no need to hedge the short. But this can often be done so that the downside potential is not significantly diminished while the upside risk is greatly reduced.

The best way to identify an undervalued warrant is to

evaluate the historical price relationship between the warrant and the optioned stock. Temporary technical weakness in a warrant can often be identified by plotting on graph paper or maintaining a chart that depicts the warrant and stock prices as they relate to predicted warrant prices. Also, you may observe that a warrant is selling at a much lower premium than before, and yet the stock price is about the same, so that the warrant may be undervalued. The preferable way to relate current prices to historical prices is to express both in terms of a normal or predicted warrant price. In terms of Figure 5–1 this implies that you must compute S/E and W/E. Then you can plot the actual prices versus the expected or normal price. To illustrate, Figure 6–1 contains a price history for Continental Telephone, using the same data as was used in Figure 3–2.

The "W/E actual" is obtained by dividing the actual warrant price by the per share exercise price. Therefore, for the first entry 0.335 is obtained by the quotient 7.50/22.38. The predicted W/E is obtained from the table in Figure 5–1. Again, for the first price we see that S/E being 1.06, we are interested in a predicted W/E that ranges between 0.42 and 0.48. The difference between these two is 0.06 and since we want to move six tenths up from $S/E = 1.00$ to reach 1.06 we have predicted W/E as 0.42 plus 0.036 or 0.456. The table is represented graphically in Figure 6–2.

Here the relationship between the actual W/E and the predicted W/E is easily seen. At the beginning of Figure 6–2 you will observe that the predicted warrant price moved sharply down towards the actual price, reflecting a drop in the common as shown in Figure 6–1. Then, from May 1, 1970 through August 21, 1970 the actual and predicted warrant prices moved in parallel, with the actual warrant being under-valued in relation to the predicted line. On September 4,

1970 the two lines diverged, with the difference between them representing the magnitude of the undervaluation. At this point the warrant stood at \$6.88 and it was a good buy or hedge candidate. Of course, in retrospect, it was a better

FIGURE 6–1
Continental Telephone (April 1970–March 1971)

Stock	Warrant	S/E	W/E Actual	W/E Predicted
23.75	7.50	1.06	0.335	0.456
21.63	6.88	0.97	0.307	0.396
19.75 (5/1/70)	5.63	0.88	0.252	0.324
19.75	5.88	0.88	0.263	0.324
19.88	6.25	0.89	0.279	0.332
19.25	6.25	0.86	0.279	0.308
18.63	5.50	0.83	0.246	0.284
20.00	6.00	0.89	0.268	0.332
19.75	6.13	0.88	0.274	0.324
19.25	5.63	0.86	0.252	0.308
19.88	6.25	0.89	0.279	0.332
22.13 (9/4/70)	6.88	0.99	0.307	0.412
22.25	6.75	0.99	0.302	0.412
22.38	6.75	1.00	0.302	0.420
22.88	6.88	1.02	0.307	0.432
22.75	7.00	1.02	0.313	0.432
23.63	7.25	1.06	0.324	0.456
24.88	7.38	1.11	0.330	0.485
25.38	8.13	1.13	0.363	0.495
25.25	7.75	1.13	0.346	0.495
25.63	8.88	1.15	0.397	0.505
26.00	9.25	1.16	0.413	0.510
26.63	9.13	1.19	0.408	0.525

Exercise price = \$22.38 per share.

buy at \$5.25, but the absolute bottom can never be predicted with any real assurance. If the warrant had been picked up at the \$6.88 level and sold at, let us say, the \$8.88 level four months later, a nice 29 percent profit (87 percent annualized) would have been realized. However, it may have been more

FIGURE 6–2

Continental Telephone Actual Warrant versus Normal Warrant Prices

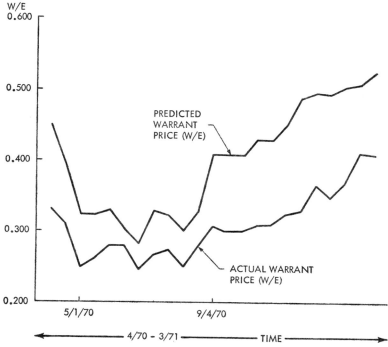

desirable to hedge the position by shorting stock. The important consideration in the beginning is to be able to identify an undervalued warrant. This is best done as in Figure 6–1 and Figure 6–2. When nice parallel channels are interrupted, it is time to take a look at the technically undervalued warrant. Data over a period of years is preferable to a small span as in the illustration.

Whenever a warrant suddenly becomes technically undervalued (or more undervalued than it was previously), it is worth investigating to see if there is some fundamental explanation. A higher predicted value may not be entirely valid if the company has just declared an unusually high dividend, or announced a new corporate development beneficial to shareholders, but not warrantholders. Since Figure 5–1 represents normal prices for the typical warrant, it is more important to observe the predicted *W/E* versus the actual *W/E* as they relate to each other over time than to compare actual to predicted at a given point in time. A warrant, being untypical, may always be undervalued or overvalued in relation to its predicted price. What is significant is a change from the historical trend. If there is no recent corporate action to explain a change, then the warrant can be considered to be technically undervalued.

SELECTING THE HEDGE RATIO

The decision to hold a hedge position instead of a straight long warrant position is one that reduces the risk and limits the reward. The ratio of warrants long to stock short is determined by the risks you can endure and the reward you seek. Unfortunately, this is a tradeoff situation. The bigger the reward you seek, the greater the risk you must endure.

Let us take a look at Continental Telephone (CTC) in Figure 6–2 as of September 4, 1970. At that point the stock stood at $22.13 (see Figure 6–1) and the warrant was at $6.88. In order to quantify the possible risk-reward combinations we must pick some stock prices below and above the current market and make some predictions as to where the warrant would be at those future prices. The easy approach would be to compute the normal warrant price (*W/E*) for assumed stock prices, the hope being that the warrant will eventually tend to sell at its normal price. However, a more appropriate assumption would be that the normal warrant price and the actual warrant price will be realigned with the same percentage difference between them that has historically been the case. Therefore, for CTC, the channel defined by the dates May 1, 1970 through August 21, 1970 in Figures 6–1 and 6–2 illustrates about a 10 percent deviation from norm. That is, the warrant sold at about 10 percent below the predicted normal price. It was reasonable to assume on September 4, 1970 that this relationship would be reestablished, hopefully at a higher warrant price. It is usually appropriate to assume a stock price range from 40 percent below to 40 percent above the market price. Figure 6–3 illustrates how you might evaluate the CTC hedge using this price range, shown in column *a*, from $15 to $30.

There are a lot of reasons why this is a safe range in general and for CTC in particular. In general, you do not plan a hedge position for a move of more than 40 percent. You will be out before then, since at most ratios either a loss will be developing before 40 percent is reached or alignment of normal and actual prices will have taken place, signalling an exit. For CTC in particular, the reasoning is simple. It is a utility which as a class of companies is not prone to huge swings. At the time its earnings were steadily improving, suggesting an upside move although stocks and money market conditions were shaky. Of course higher interest rates hurt utilities since large investments are required (debt financing) to grow. At the time the common was yielding 3.6 percent on the dividend, limiting the downside risk somewhat. Also, utility earnings tend to hold up in recessionary periods. Following this type of reasoning, you can easily select the range of stock prices to be considered.

At the selected stock prices S/E is calculated (column *b*). Using the S/E values, Figure 5–1 provides the corresponding, predicted W/E (column *c*). Columns *d* and *e* convert each predicted W/E into predicted normal warrant price and 90

FIGURE 6-3
Continental Telephone Hedge Analysis

(a)	(b)	(c)	(d)	(e)	(f)	(g)	(h)
						Potential Gain or Loss	
Stock	S/E	Predicted W/E	Predicted Warrant	90% Predicted Warrant	Buy	2-1 Hedge	3-1 Hedge
$15.00	0.67	0.19	$ 4.25	$ 3.83	(44)%	8%	(10)%
16.00	0.71	0.21	4.70	4.23	(39)	6	(9)
17.00	0.76	0.24	5.37	4.83	(30)	7	(5)
18.00	0.80	0.26	5.82	5.24	(24)	6	(4)
19.00	0.85	0.30	6.72	6.05	(12)	11	3
20.00	0.89	0.33	7.39	6.65	(3)	12	7
21.00	0.94	0.37	8.06	7.25	5	14	11
22.00	0.98	0.40	8.95	8.06	17	18	18
23.00	1.03	0.44	9.85	8.86	29	22	25
24.00	1.07	0.46	10.30	9.27	35	21	26
25.00	1.12	0.49	10.97	9.87	44	23	30
26.00	1.16	0.51	11.41	10.27	49	21	31
27.00	1.21	0.54	12.08	10.87	58	23	34
28.00	1.25	0.58	12.98	11.68	70	27	41
29.00	1.30	0.62	13.88	12.49	82	32	48
30.00	1.34	0.65	14.55	13.09	90	33	52

Exercise price (E) = $22.38.
Stock on 9/4/70 = $22.13.
Warrant on 9/4/70 = $ 6.88.

percent of same, respectively. Therefore, we would expect, using column *e,* that if the stock dropped to $15.00, the warrant would move to about $3.83. On the upside a move to $30.00 on the common is expected to result in a $13.09 warrant price.

In calculating the gain or loss, actual or predicted, on a hedge position, using Reg T but not considering buying on margin, the following arithmetic relations are useful:

1. For an actual position held:

   Gain (loss) =
   [(number of warrants long) (warrant price sold
   — warrant price bought) + (number of shares sold)
   (stock price sold — stock price bought)]/ (number of
   warrants long) (warrant price bought)

2. For a predicted position:

   Gain (loss) predicted =
   [(number of warrants long) (warrant price future
   — warrant price now) + (number of shares sold)
   (stock price now — stock price future)]/ (number of
   warrants long) (warrant price now)

Using Reg T, column *f* depicts the profit possible as a result of a straight warrant purchase. Columns *g* and *h* illustrate the results for a two-to-one and three-to-one hedge, respectively. The first line shows the predicted results if the stock should have fallen to $15.00. On a straight buy a loss of 44 percent develops; that is, there is a loss of $305 in the warrant position ($688 less $383) and this is 44 percent of the required investment of $688. On a two-to-one hedge, only the $1,376 ($688 times 2 since we are long 200 warrants) need be put up. Here a $610 loss ($305 times 2) is expected in the warrant position, but the 100 short common shares would yield a profit of $713 ($2,213 less $1,500). The net gain is $103 yielding an 8 percent profit ($103 divided by $1,376).

FIGURE 6–4
Continental Telephone (CTC) Profit Profile—Hedges—

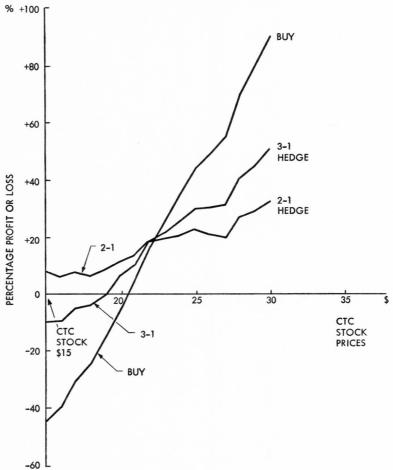

On the three-to-one hedge we would expect a poorer result on the extreme downside, and it is a 10 percent loss with a required investment of $2,064 and a loss of $202. Although Figure 6–3 tells the story, Figure 6–4 is an even better method of representing the predictions.

First, you will recognize that at about $22 the three lines come together, reflecting the even profit distribution of about 15 percent across the three positions on the corresponding line in Figure 6–3. At stock prices below the then current stock price of $22.13, the buy is the riskiest, producing the greatest losses. The two-to-one hedge is the most conservative of the three positions, yielding an expected gain of 8 percent on the extreme downside, but also having only a 33 percent expected gain on the upside. A lower ratio (one warrant long for each share short) would be more conservative. Ratios higher than three-to-one would increase risk and reward, pushing the three-to-one line (as it is now) closer to the "buy" line.

Our original hypothesis was that the selection of the appropriate hedge ratio was contingent upon the risks and rewards. Figure 6–4 illustrates these. The slope (steepness) of the lines illustrates the risk-reward matrix over the illustrated range of possible stock prices. Another way of showing this risk-reward matrix is to transform Figure 6–4 into some boxes, as has been done in Figure 6–5.

Each box outlines the area described by the line which is its left-to-right diagonal. The height of a given box above the zero profit line represents the potential reward. The depth below the line is the potential loss, that is, the risk. The ratio of depth to height can be considered the risk-reward ratio. For each possible position we have:

Position	Risk-Reward Ratio
Buy	0.622
3-to-1 hedge	0.423
2-to-1 hedge	0.121

There are many other arithmetic and graphic (such as relating slopes, areas of boxes, and probabilities of stock

Uncommon Profits through Stock Purchase Warrants

FIGURE 6–5

Continental Telephone (CTC) Profit Profile—Hedges—

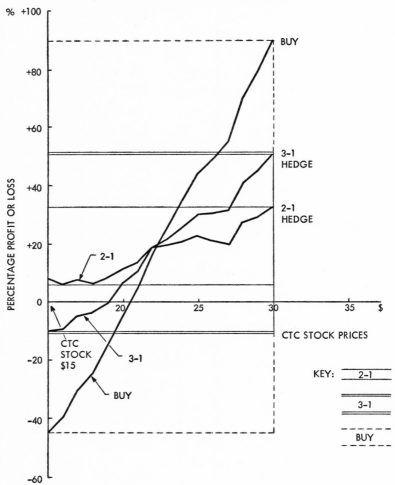

drops) methods of computing a risk-reward matrix. No one is better than another. What is important is that you attempt to measure this by some method, and then consistently use that method. Through this experience you will gain an appreciation for the relative merits of different ratios for a given hedge position and the ability to evaluate one candidate against another.

WHEN TO CLOSE A WARRANT HEDGE

A warrant hedge position should be closed in the case of any of the following conditions:

1. Warrant has returned to a normal price.
2. Objectives have been accomplished with respect to gain.
3. Constraint has been broken on loss side.
4. An unusual corporate development has taken place.

By far the most significant condition that we look for is a revaluation of the warrant by the marketplace such that it is no longer technically underpriced. This adjustment to a more normal price may result in a profit or a loss. In either case the position should be closed.

If your profit objectives have been met, why keep a position open? Only if the position, its potential, and risk-reward profile still looks better than any other alternative investment you might have, should you keep it open. Just because a hedge has worked out well does not mean it will continue to do so. A decision to stay in after profit objectives have been met is equivalent to closing and reopening the position mentally, with the benefit of no commissions.

When a risk rule or constraint has been violated, close the hedge position. Taking the loss that you and your conscience agreed to risk when you entered the position is far more preferable (and less costly) to "hanging in there," hoping for relief. Professionals close losing positions at a predetermined level of loss. Amateurs ride them into the dust. Taking the emotion out of your buy and sell criteria is a major step toward successful investing.

Occasionally there will be little or no change in a hedge position, but a dramatic corporate announcement suggests that it should be closed or modified. You may want to get a jump on bad news and close the position quickly. If the news is very favorable and the warrant has not moved yet and therefore is still significantly underpriced, you may want to double up on the warrant side.

7

Expiring Warrants—
Fortunes to be Made

W HEN A WARRANT expires it must trade at or a mere fraction below its intrinsic value. If it has a negative intrinsic value, then an expiring warrant tends to trade at one
eighth or so near expiration. However, until a short period
before expiration warrants tend to trade at a premium. Warrants are purchased to obtain leverage, and, as expiration
approaches, the warrantholder has less and less time to benefit from the leverage that could produce substantial profits
based on an upside optioned stock move. For this reason the
premiums paid for expiring warrants diminish almost in a
direct relationship with the ebbing life left. Knowing that a
warrant must sell at or close to its intrinsic value upon expiration, the warrant trader hopes to take advantage of the current
premium paid. Specifically, shorting expiring warrants can
be a very profitable game. You can also hedge the short by
simultaneously buying some optioned stock. When you hold

FIGURE 7–1
Profit Profile for Short Sale of Expiring Warrant

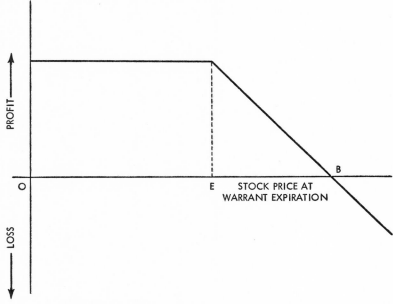

E is final per share exercise price.

stock and are short warrants, you are in a *reverse hedge* position. Herein lies the real profit power in warrant trading. It is possible to establish positions that are potentially highly profitable with little risk exposure.

THE SHORT SIDE

When selling an expiring warrant short, you hope that it sells at or near its intrinsic value upon expiration. Ideally this final price is at or near zero, since you would like to short only those warrants with large, negative intrinsic values. Let us take an example: A warrant calls common at $6 per share and sells at $2 while the stock is $4 a year before warrant expiration. If you short the warrants at $2, your hope is that they will be near zero in a year. Your risk is easily determined since the warrant will trade at zero upon expiration as long as the stock is at or below $6 at that point. You would enjoy a maximum profit if the stock is at or below the final exercise price upon expiration. A loss would develop only if the stock were above $8 upon warrant expiration. At this price the warrant would have an intrinsic value of $2. In general a loss develops when the stock rises above the final exercise price in an amount equal to the price where the warrants were shorted.

The above concept associated with selling short expiring warrants is easily depicted on a profit diagram as illustrated in Figure 7–1.

This diagram shows the profit possibilities of shorting expiring warrants which sell at a premium and covering the short sale upon expiration at a price equivalent to the warrant's intrinsic value or zero, whichever is higher. For all optioned stock prices from zero to E the profit potential is constant. This follows since the warrant will tend to trade at zero as long as the optioned stock is below the effective per share exercise price. If the optioned stock sells for more than E, then profits diminish and a loss begins to develop beyond the break-even point B. At point B the stock sells at a price such that the warrant's intrinsic value equals the price at which the warrants were shorted. As is evident the risk in a warrant short on an expiring warrant with no intrinsic value is on an upside optioned stock move. On the downside one couldn't care less if the stock goes to zero!

REVERSING THE RISK

While the straight short sale of an expiring warrant places the risk on an upside stock move, a *one-to-one reverse hedge* places the risk on a downside stock move. Here you purchase a number of shares equal to the shares called by the shorted warrants. If each warrant calls 1.05 shares of stock, then you purchase 105 shares for each 100 warrants short. Returning to the earlier example, where the stock sells at $4 while the warrant is at $2 on a final exercise price of $6, it is evident that a one-to-one reverse hedge results in a profit as long as the stock sells at or above $6 upon expiration. At successively higher stock prices the loss on the warrant short is offset by the gain on the stock. Suppose the stock sold at $6 upon expiration. At this point there would be a $2 gain on the stock purchase and a $2 gain on the warrant short giving a gain of $4 or roughly a 67 percent profit over the life of the position. At a stock price of $10 the net profit would be the same since on the long stock side a $6 gain would be realized, but on the warrant short side the loss would be $2, for a net gain of $4. This shortside loss develops because the warrant would sell at its intrinsic value of $4 with the stock at $10 and the warrant was shorted at $2. The cost to cover the short is therefore $2. Figure 7–2 illustrates this reversal of the risk and it is clearly the antithesis of Figure 7–1.

Here the risk is on the downside with constant profits when the stock is at or above *E* upon warrant expiration. Below *E*, profits diminish until at point *A* a loss develops. In this example this would be at a stock price of $2, where the loss on the stock long position of $2 would be offset by the gain on the warrant short, also $2.

Most investors, dealing with imperfect information, do not wish to place all of the risk on one side of a stock move, either down or up. By combining the straight short and the one-to-one reverse hedge it is possible to increase the potential profit in expiring warrants while spreading the risk across both sides of the final exercise price.

FIGURE 7–2

Profit Profile for One-to-one Reverse Hedge in Expiring Warrant

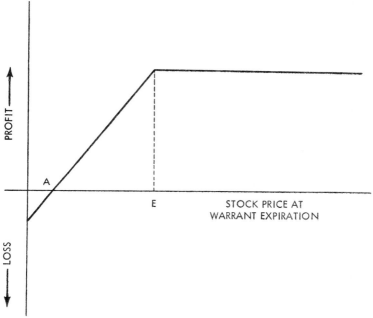

UNBALANCED REVERSE HEDGE

A technique that combines the short sale of expiring warrants method with the one-to-one reverse hedge is the *unbalanced reverse hedge,* commonly called the "many-to-one
reverse hedge" where many is replaced by the appropriate
number. Looking at it in another way, the technique requires
that you buy a lesser number of shares than called by the
shorted warrants. If you enter into a three-to-one reverse
hedge, then you purchase one share of stock for each three
warrants shorted. The many-to-one reverse hedge can be com-

pared and related to the previously discussed one-to-one reverse hedge as follows:

1. It is potentially more profitable.
2. It places the risk on both sides of the effective exercise price.
3. It narrows the stock price range within which profits are possible.

The tradeoff is obvious—a higher risk (narrower profit range of stock prices) for a greater potential reward.

Historical examples of successful reverse hedges just abound! Making profits with this technique is not a paper exercise, but a very practical and real occurrence.

The Jefferson Lake Petrochemicals of Canada (JLP) warrant, traded on the Toronto Stock Exchange (TOR) on April 30, 1970 at \$3.00 while the stock stood at \$10.50. Each warrant represented the right to buy 1.0608 shares of common at \$13.00 per share until June 1, 1971. With the stock selling at less than the exercise price ($S/E = 10.50/13.00$ or 0.81), the expiring warrant presented an ideal reverse hedge situation. Unless the stock rose to 13.00 ($S/E = 1.0$) by June 1, 1971, the warrant had to sell almost at zero on that date. Thus in 13 months the stock had to move \$2.50 or 24 percent before the expiring warrant would have intrinsic value, and moreover, remain at or above that level through June 1, 1971. Although the oils have always been volatile, the risk-reward ratio seemed favorable in light of the firm's then-recent earnings record.

Suppose that on April 30, 1970 you felt that a straight short in the JLP warrant was too risky, but that a three-to-one reverse hedge was appropriate. Actually your ratio would have been slightly less than three-to-one since each warrant called 1.0608 shares. However, since it is easier to short a round lot of 300 warrants than it is an odd lot of 283 (the number required for a pure three-to-one reverse hedge) you would probably go with the 300 warrants short. If you had entered into this position at that time you would have done so with a lot of company as evidenced by the rising short position in the warrant as reported by the Toronto Stock Exchange during that period. Figure 7–3 illustrates how you would have been positioned on April 30, 1970. As shown, the maximum unmargined profit is obtained if the warrant sells at the effective exercise price of $13.00 at expiration.

Here the potential profit is 59 percent. The risk is partially expressed in terms of the stock prices below and above which a loss develops. If the stock sells down to $1.50, then there is a $9.00 loss on the long common side which is offset by the equal profit when the warrant is covered at zero (3 times $3). At a stock price of $18.30 a loss again develops, as the profit in the long stock position of $7.80 is offset by the equivalent loss in the warrants. At a stock price of $18.30, each warrant is worth about $5.60 ($18.30 less $13.00, which is the per share exercise price, times 1.0608 which is the number of shares called). Since warrants were shorted at $3.00, the total loss is $2.60 per warrant or $7.80 for each three warrants short. As Figure 7–3 aptly illustrates, the position promised a profit for a stock range of $1.50 to $18.30 while the stock stood at $10.50. This represented profit coverage for a —86 percent to +74 percent swing in the stock. How many investments can you think of where you do not care if the stock is cut by 86 percent or increases by 74 percent, because you will still make money? More significantly, how often have you entered a position where you hoped that the stock remained about the same (maximum

FIGURE 7–3

Profit Potential JLP Warrant View on April 30, 1970, Three-to-one Reverse Hedge

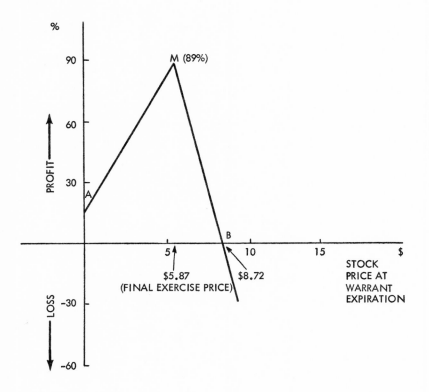

profit occurs if the stock sells at the exercise price upon expiration)? Incidentally, the probability that a given issue will be close to (±20 percent) its present price two years from now is a lot greater than that it will be a long way (±75 percent or more) from its current price.

Let us take a look at another, historical example. On February 26, 1971 the ASE-listed warrants of First National Realty

& Construction Corp. (FNR) sold at $1.50, while the stock stood at $3.38. Each warrant called 1.15 shares of common at $5.87 per share until December 31, 1971. In February the short position in the warrant stood at 109,000 out of a total of 540,000, so there were still plenty around for short purposes. This fact is further verified in that when the ASE banned further short sales in May there were 148,000 warrants short, almost 40,000 more than a few weeks earlier. A very desirable reverse hedge was available. FNR was experiencing losses and the outlook was dim. It was unlikely that the stock would move significantly in the next 10 months. With an S/E of 0.58 the situation was favorable. The profit potential of a three-to-one reverse hedge is shown in Figure 7–4.

Here the maximum profit of 89 percent occurs if the stock is at $5.87 upon warrant expiration. At that point there would have been a $1.50 profit on each warrant short and a $2.49 profit on each common share long. Thus the maximum potential profit was $4.50 (3 warrants short) plus $2.49 or $6.99 on an investment of $7.88, yielding the 89 percent. As Figure 7–4 demonstrates, there would have been a 14 percent profit even if the stock sold down to zero! At this point the loss on the stock is more than offset by the gain of $4.50 on the warrants short. On the upside the breakeven point (B) is at a stock price of $8.72. Beyond that point the three-to-one hedge would result in a loss. For FNR the range of protection was $0 to $8.72 with a maximum profit of 89 percent (this is 107 percent annualized). The upside risk was significantly reduced by the poor earnings and earnings projections for the next year.

Suppose you had entered into these two reverse hedge positions. It is interesting to see how you would have fared. On May 28, 1971 the JLP warrant traded for 3 cents with

FIGURE 7–4

Profit Potential FNR Warrant View on February 26, 1971, Three-to-one Reverse Hedge

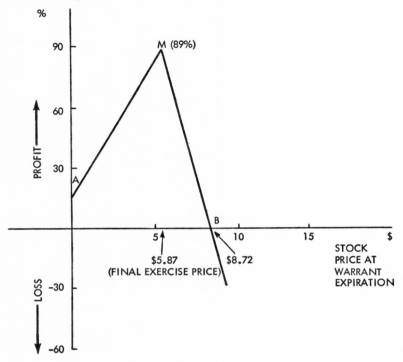

the stock at $10.87. At that point a profit of $8.91 in the warrant short position was realized along with a 37 cent profit on each stock purchased. The actual profit was 48 percent.

On December 23, 1971, the last day it traded on the American Stock Exchange, the FNR warrant traded at one sixty-fourth, or about 2 cents, while stock traded at $1.38. In this position a 31 percent profit was enjoyed.

These are only two examples of the many that have been available in recent years. With many new warrants being issued, such opportunities should continue to exist in the future.

IDENTIFYING REVERSE HEDGE CANDIDATES

At first thought it might appear to be a horrendous job to isolate the few warrants that are reverse hedge candidates from the hundreds that trade in the various markets. However, the rules for this identification process make the job quite easy. In order to qualify as a candidate a warrant must: (1) be listed on an exchange; (2) sell for more than 50 cents; (3) have less than 36 months to go prior to expiration; (4) have little or no intrinsic value (based on the final exercise price); (5) have a minimum float of 100,000 warrants; and (6) be shortable.

These rules are designed to produce a master list of candidates from which the most profitable, least risky positions should be considered. A compilation of all listed warrants can be obtained by scanning the newspaper quotation section for all major exchanges or consulting a reputable warrant service. This list can be reduced by eliminating all warrants selling for less than 50 cents. The terms and facts for the warrant must be available for further culling. These are available from the company, your broker, or a reputable warrant service. The cutoff point of 36 months before expiration is one that, based on historical data, is most opportune for first examining a warrant for reverse hedge possibilities. There is a tradeoff in that the further away from expiration, the greater the risk and the lesser the potential annualized profit is, while as expiration approaches the warrant premium is chopped as hopes for long position profits diminish. In computing intrinsic value it is important to use the final exercise price if it differs from the current. A step-up in exercise price or a bond's becoming usable can cause this difference. We are concerned with what the warrant's value is at expiration. This is best expressed by computing S/E where E is the final exercise price. Any value over 1.0 should be viewed skeptically. If there are less than 100,000 warrants outstanding, then there is a thin market and covering your short may be a problem. For this reason small warrant issues should be avoided. A listed warrant is shortable if it can be borrowed and the exchange has not banned short sales.

If you performed this identification task on July 30, 1971, you would have come up with a list identical to the one in Figure 7–5.

This list is the basis for further study.

CHOOSING THE MIX

As Figure 7–5 suggests, one measure of risk is the S/E which indicates how far the stock must travel so that the final exercise price and stock price are equal ($S/E = 1.0$) upon warrant expiration. Based on this criteria alone, it would appear that Lectro Management ($S/E = 0.28$) and Elgin National Industries ($S/E = 0.30$) offered the lowest risk profile in July of 1971, while, of those considered with S/E less than 1.0, Husky Oil and United Canso offered the highest risk ($S/E = 0.99$). However, there is one dimension of risk which the S/E figure neglects, and that is time. It is more probable that the average security on any exchange will double in a year than that it will double in six months. The longer your horizon, the less certain you can be in predicting. As a result, time to expiration is a critical factor in evaluating the risk of a warrant moving from a current S/E which is less than 1.0 to an S/E of 1.0. Of course you can measure this risk

FIGURE 7–5
Reverse Hedge Candidates, July 30, 1971

Exchange	Warrant	Warrant Price	Months to Expiration	S/E (final)	Float (thousands)
ASE	Atlantic Richfield	$4.13	13	0.60	500
PC	Avco Community Dev.	2.88	29	0.77	123
ASE	Bluebird	3.13	32	0.59	600
TOR	Canada Southern Pete.	2.95	29	0.98	618
ASE	Elgin Nat'l Indust.	1.63	28	0.30	900
TOR	Gaz Metropolitain '63	2.17	22	0.96	428
TOR	Houston Oils	1.11	17	0.68	300
TOR	Husky Oil	7.35	35	0.99	297
NTL	Lectro Management	0.75	10	0.28	105
PC	Magellan Pete.	1.00	5	0.79	409
TOR	Markborough Properties	1.05	12	0.71	300
ASE	Republic Mortgage Inv.	5.13	35	0.96	1,064
PC	Texas Int'l Pete.	4.88	34	0.89	450
TOR	Traders Group '65	2.25	16	0.93	250
TOR	United Canso Oil & Gas	1.83	8	0.99	244
TOR	White Pass & Yukon	1.70	18	0.41	110

Exchange Key:
  ASE = American
  NTL = National
  PC = Pacific Coast
  TOR = Toronto

in many cases. If a firm is in deep trouble and presents a prospect of little or no recovery in the future (up to expiration), then you might be able to live with a higher S/E than if the firm appeared poised for recovery.

For a given ratio of warrants short to optioned stock long, you would be interested in knowing how much per month the stock could move between now and expiration before a loss develops. In our previous examples of the Jefferson Lake (JLP) and First National Realty (FNR) reverse hedges we calculated stock price points below (A) and above which (B) a loss developed if the stock sold at those prices upon warrant expiration. At the point of position entry on JLP the stock

FIGURE 7–6

Profit Potential and Breakeven Points for JLP Reverse Hedge Ratios, April 30, 1970

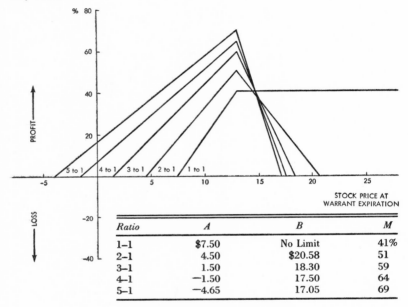

Ratio	A	B	M
1–1	$7.50	No Limit	41%
2–1	4.50	$20.58	51
3–1	1.50	18.30	59
4–1	−1.50	17.50	64
5–1	−4.65	17.05	69

A = Breakeven stock price downside.
B = Breakeven stock price upside.
M = Maximum Profit Percent Possible.

stood at $10.50 and the breakeven points for the three-to-one ratio were $1.50 and $18.30, respectively, with 13 months to go on the warrant. Therefore the stock had to fall $9.00 in 13 months or 6.9 percent per month before a loss developed on the downside. On the upside the stock had to move 6.0 percent per month before a loss developed. This is the real measure of risk. When evaluating a position you must ask yourself if the stock can move at the rate suggested. If you think it can, then you may wish to alter the risk.

Risk in reverse hedges is shifted by changing the ratio of warrants short to stock long. A higher ratio increases risk;

a lower ratio reduces risk. This is best illustrated graphically, as in Figure 7–6.

Here the breakeven points for various ratios in the JLP situation are illustrated. The three-to-one profit triangle is a replica of what is in Figure 7–3. Notice that even at ratios higher than three-to-one the downside breakeven point (*A*) is a negative number and therefore, since zero is the practical lower limit, there is no danger of a loss developing on the downside. However at the higher ratios the upside breakeven point (*B*) moves lower, increasing risk. The horizontal line extending out at 41 percent profit on the one-to-one ratio indicates that this profit will be held no matter how high the stock goes. Here the profit is the current premium and subsequent losses on each warrant short are equalized by the stock long.

Points *A* and *B* are easily calculated using the formulas in Figure 7–7.

When you are dealing with warrants which call an even number of shares, the use of these formulas is quite simple. However, as in the case of JLP, when the number of shares called by the warrant has a fractional part, care must be used. Let us illustrate the use of these for JLP at three to one. The warrant called 1.0608 shares at $13.00 per share with the stock at $10.50 and the warrants at $3.00. Breakeven point *A* is calculated, approximately since *R* has been rounded, as:

$$A = \$10.50 - (3.1824)(2.83)$$
$$A = \$10.50 - 9.00$$
$$A = \$1.50$$

Here the *R* factor is 1.0608 times three or 3.1824 since each warrant calls 1.0608 shares. The adjusted warrant price is $3 divided by the same 1.0608 or about $2.83. Breakeven

FIGURE 7–7
Breakeven Point Calculations

$$A = S - RW$$
$$B = \frac{R(W + E) - S}{R - 1}$$

Where:

S = The price at which the optioned stock is purchased.

W = The adjusted warrant price (price of a call on one share) at which the warrants are shorted.

R = The ratio of the number of shares called by the shorted warrants to the number of shares purchased.

E = The effective per share exercise price at expiration.

point B is calculated, approximately since R has been rounded, as:

$$B = \$[3.1824\ (2.83 + 13.00) - 10.50]/2.1824$$
$$B = \$18.30 \text{ (approximate)}$$

A similar application of these formulas for different ratios results in the numbers shown in Figure 7–6. One could also calculate the percent per month by which the issue must change to reach points A and B for each ratio.

It would be most helpful if, for those candidates in Figure 7–5, one could illustrate for various ratios the breakeven points and the percent change per month in the stock price required to reach those points. This could be done graphically, as in Figure 7–6. However, with a long list of warrants the graph would become cluttered. For comparative purposes a tabular presentation is more informative as shown in the Appendix. Now risks can be compared, both between ratios for a given warrant and between warrants. Take a look at Canada Southern Petroleum. At ratios higher than one-to-one there is no downside risk of a loss since point A is negative. On the upside, however, the risk profile changes with ratio changes. At two-to-one the stock must move up 4 percent per month until expiration in order for a loss to develop. However, at ratios higher than three-to-one the upside risk does not change, requiring a 2 percent move per month up in the stock in order to result in breakeven. This suggests that if you are willing to go to four-to-one, the added risk of going to nine-to-one or more is minimal. Scanning the list, you find that Lectro Management appears to offer the lowest risk profile. At four-to-one, as an example, the stock must go up a total of 376 percent, or 37 percent per month in the 10 months until expiration before a loss develops. On the downside a loss is not possible. Others that look favorable are Elgin, Houston Oils, Magellan, and White Pass. However, this is only a view of the risks. In order to select the proper candidates at the proper ratio, you must evaluate risk in light of potential rewards.

So far the extent of the reward evaluation has been the evaluation of profits for various ratios as illustrated in Figure 7–6. The maximum reward (profit) for any given ratio is found at the apex (point *M*) where the stock sells at the exercise price upon expiration. At other stock prices the reward is read off the line depicted for the desired ratio. In evaluating potential profits, you would be unreasonable to assume (and select candidates on this basis) that the stock will sell at the exercise price some months hence at warrant expiration. If *S/E* is very low and corporate prospects are bad, the probability of such a recovery is quite slim. The only logical assumption to make is that the stock will sell right where it is now at warrant expiration. This is the most probable event. It will not in all likelihood sell at exactly the current price, but it will be closer to its current price than any other price you might pick. Therefore the desired measure of comparison for a given warrant (different ratios) and between warrants is the probable profit. This is calculated assuming the same stock price at expiration. As long as S/E is less than or equal to 1.0 to start with, the probable profit percentage is merely the warrant price multiplied by the ratio divided by the investment. The appendix depicts the probable profit at various ratios for each warrant. Notice that there are two calculations made. First, the actual percentage is shown. For example, Avco Community Developers shows an actual probable profit of 84 percent at six-to-one, but this is only 35 percent on an annual basis since the warrant has 29 months to go to expiration. However, United Canso's 114 percent probable profit at six-to-one looks a lot better annualized to 171 percent, reflecting less than a year to go to expiration. The only valid way to compare probable profits is on an annualized basis. The goal is to keep your money working at the highest possible annual return. Clearly a 50 percent return in one year is far superior to the same gain in two years.

At this point you have the tools to select the candidates and ratios from the list in Figure 7–5. These tools are illustrated in the Appendix. At this point you may feel that the creation of these analytical tools (numbers) would be quite laborious. On the contrary, using a calculator, you may quickly dispatch the task. If you have access to a computer, all the better. A weekend invested in such an activity should be well worth it in light of the probable and potential rewards.

The evaluation of the risks and rewards is not purely mechanical. It is a very personal activity. Why don't you compile your list, in order of preference, and compare it to another view as shown in Figure 7–8?

The major risk factors were considered against the probable rewards. The averages for the eight warrants selected are quite interesting. The S/E is well below 1.0 at 0.76. The average amount that the stocks must move up is 10 percent

FIGURE 7–8
Selected Reverse Hedge Positions* (as of July 30, 1971)

Warrant	Ratio	S/E	Upside Risk**	Probable Profit	
				Actual	Annual
Magellan Pete.	4–1	0.79	14%	32%	76%
United Canso	5–1	0.99	6	108	162
Houston Oils	4–1	0.99	8	79	57
White Pass & Yukon	6–1	0.41	11	73	49
Lectro Management	9–1	0.28	28	28	33
Markborough	4–1	0.71	7	63	63
Gaz '63	4–1	0.96	3	120	65
Canada South Pete.	3–1	0.98	3	122	50
Averages		0.76	10	78	69

* Selected using Figure 7–5 and the Appendix.
** The percentage per month by which the stock must advance before a loss is possible at expiration.

per month or a full 120 percent per year. This is not likely under even the most explosive market conditions. The probable annual profit is 69 percent; not bad when weighed against the risks. At this point some time has passed since the list was compiled in July of 1971. Some or all of the warrants may have expired. Why don't you consult your broker, get current or last day of warrant trading prices, and see how you might have done with your list or the one in Figure 7–8?

USING MARGIN TO INCREASE PROFITS

Since the profit on any completed position is calculated as the net change in the position divided by the investment, it is desirable to minimize the investment required to carry a position. Buying on margin means that the investor puts up less than the face amount of any given transaction. The difference between the market value and the amount you put up is borrowed from your broker. This creates a debit in your account and you pay interest on this. In short, buying on margin is a technique that enables the investor to have more money working for him than he has had to put up himself.

Most people have a general brokerage account which consists of three subaccounts: cash, margin, and short. The cash account holds those securities which you paid for in full. They may be registered in your name, as opposed to *street name* meaning, "in the name of your broker." Securities that are purchased on margin or that are being held by your broker as collateral against margin loans are held in the margin account. These securities are registered in street name so your broker can lend them to other brokers (for short selling) or use them as collateral to borrow. The short account records those securities you have sold short.

When you sell short, your broker borrows the securities from someone else's margin account, sells them, and simultaneously debits and credits your short account for the net proceeds of the sale. The debit indicates that you are short that amount of stock and it completely offsets the credit which represents the cash proceeds of the short sale. This credit balance is not available to you until the short position is closed. It just sits alongside the debit in the short account. If the broker did not have to go outside his own house to borrow the shorted securities, then this credit balance is available to your house.

Minimum margin requirements are set by the Federal Reserve System (FRS). These rates infrequently change to reflect the FRS monetary policy decisions. At this writing the margin rate is 55 percent. On a straight purchase you must post at least 55 percent of the purchase price. The remaining amount, up to 45 percent, is lent to you at interest by your broker. When selling short, you must also post at least 55 percent of the short sale value to demonstrate your good faith;

that is, that you will at some point cover the short position. However, you do not borrow the difference in the case of a short. Therefore on short sales there are no interest charges. In fact the *good faith money* that you put up (55 percent) to support the short position is transferred to your margin account where it reduces current debit balances (and therefore, as a consequence, interest charges). As a result, short selling has a side benefit in that it adds credit to your margin account and has the effect of reducing carrying charges.

All of the above is quite significant to the warrant trader who executes a reverse hedge. The optioned stock can be bought on margin by putting up 55 percent of the purchase price. The warrants sold short must be backed up by 55 percent of the sale proceeds as good faith money. However, this good faith money can be applied against the borrowing on the margined purchase. If 55 percent of the value of the shorted warrants equals or exceeds 45 percent of the value of stock purchased, then all interest charges on the borrowed 45 percent for stock purchase are eliminated. These are the rules set by the FRS. There are, however, other margin rules that must be contended with.

The New York Stock Exchange (NYSE) sets rules which must be followed by all NYSE member firms regardless of which exchange the sale is transacted on. As shown in Figure 7–9, for low-priced securities the NYSE rules are more stringent than those of the FRS.

Canadian margin requirements are set by the Toronto Stock Exchange. The rates shown in Figure 7–9 are the current ones and, similar to NYSE rules, there is a difference between purchases and sales. The rules in Canada are less strict than in the United States on purchases of securities selling above \$1.74. On the short side, things are better all around in Canada.

FIGURE 7–9

Margin Requirements

	Purchases		*Short Sales*	
FRS	55% of value		55% of value	
NYSE	55% of value		*Market Price Shorted Security*	*Collateral Required*
			$7.70 and up	55% of value
			$5.00 to $7.69	$5.00
			$2.50 to $4.99	100% of value
			under $2.50	$2.50
TOR	*Market Price of Security*	*Minimum Margin*	*Market Price Shorted Security*	*Collateral Required*
	$2.00 and up	50%	$2.00 and up	50% of value
	$1.75 to $1.99	60%	$1.50 to $1.99	$3.00 less value
	$1.50 to $1.74	80%	$0.25 to $1.49	100% of value
	under $1.50	100%	under $0.25	$0.25

FRS = Federal Reserve System.
NYSE = New York Stock Exchange.
TOR = Toronto Stock Exchange.

After the FRS and the exchanges have had their say, your brokerage house may have still another set of rules. If these are more onerous than the NYSE minimums, then finding another broker is in order. There are many reputable brokers who use the NYSE and FRS guidelines. By the same token there are some small, non-NYSE member firms that have more lenient requirements than NYSE-member firms. However, the added risk of doing business with such a firm usually is not worth the added reward of lower margin requirements. The above U.S. requirements are called *initial margin requirements*. These are much higher than the *maintenance margin requirements* which stipulate how much must be in the account to support a previously established position. Maintenance requirements are levels that must be met over the life of a position as prices fluctuate.

The use of margin has a dramatic effect on the potential profit percentage. Take a look at the five-to-one reverse hedge for United Canso in the Appendix. With the stock at $5.20 and the warrant at $1.83 the actual probable profit is $9.15 ($1.83 times 5) on an unmargined investment of $14.35 ($5.20 plus $9.15). This amounts to 64 percent. However, when the margin requirements shown in Figure 7–9 are introduced into the picture, the actual probable profit changes. To support the short sale in the warrant, $1.17 must be put up for each warrant ($3.00 less $1.83). The total amount to support the short side is $5.85 ($1.17 times 5). The long position in the stock is supported by $2.60 (50 percent of $5.20) bringing the total investment to $8.45. Instead of a 64 percent probable profit (unannualized) we now have 108 percent. This is quite significant and, as a result, the figures in the Appendix reflect the applicable margin requirements (65 percent in the United States at that time).

TRADING CANADIAN WARRANTS

Since a large number of warrants are listed on Canadian Exchanges, U.S. residents should not be afraid to take advantage of the opportunities that exist there, especially reverse hedge opportunities. In addition, the current Canadian margin requirements are less strict on the whole than those in force in the United States, providing higher potential profit margins. However, there are some additional facts about trading Canadian securities which are important.

To discourage the outflow of dollars the U.S. government some years ago instituted the infamous "Interest Equalization Tax." This is a levy, currently at 11¼ percent which is down from more onerous numbers in the past, applicable to the purchase price of foreign securities by U.S. residents. This is a one-time tax. For example, if you, as a U.S. resident, purchase Canadian securities with a market value of $1,000, you immediately owe the U.S. Internal Revenue Service (IRS) $112.50. In fact, if executed by a U.S. broker, this amount will be deducted and paid for you at the source. Once the tax has been paid on a given certificate, however, a subsequent U.S. resident purchasing the same securities does not pay the tax. The theory here is that only the original purchase results in an outflow of dollars. Therefore there are two types of Canadian certificates available for a given security, one upon which the tax has not been paid and which trades in Canada, the other on which the tax has already been paid and which more than likely trades on a U.S. exchange or OTC. Because of this tax many Canadian exchange-listed securities also trade on U.S. exchanges and OTC. As you may have guessed, those trading in the United States with a prepaid tax usually trade at a premium over those trading in Canada. As will become evident, this tax is not as bad as it sounds for the reverse hedge trader.

As in the United States, when Canadian securities are sold short they must be borrowed by your broker and therefore must reside in someone's margin account. To be marginable in the United States a security must be listed in the United States. Most Canadian securities are not listed on U.S. exchanges. This makes borrowing difficult. Your U.S. broker cannot borrow the desired securities from a Canadian house even if it is an affiliate of the U.S. house. The most practical solution is to open an account with a Canadian brokerage house. A look at the ads in *The Financial Post* will reveal the largest ones. A few of the largest U.S. brokers have affiliates in Canada. A letter to the Toronto Stock Exchange at 234

Bay Street will also produce a list of its member firms. In any case, the larger houses in Canada are quite reputable. In addition, most Canadian brokers have telephone tie-lines to major U.S. cities or will accept collect calls, so the cost and process of opening an account is the same as it is in the United States. The only drawback is that unless you travel to Canada you do not have face-to-face knowledge of your broker. However, in the area of reverse hedges, your Canadian broker should be an order taker, not an advisor.

Trading on Canadian exchanges through a Canadian broker does not eliminate the obligation to report and pay the interest equalization tax. However, your Canadian broker will not withhold and pay it for you as is done in the United States. You must contact the IRS and obtain the proper forms for filing.

Some warrant traders split their business between the United States and Canada, purchasing certificates on which the tax has been paid in the United States and shorting securities wherever the best price is obtainable. However, in reverse hedges it is usually desirable to trade Canadian securities totally in your Canadian account. One drawback to splitting is that long securities (which can be used as collateral for borrowing in margin accounts) may not be in the proper account, increasing the necessary investment. Another reason for maintaining one account for Canadian reverse hedges is that you desire simultaneous execution of both sides in the most liquid market possible.

The 11¼ percent tax may not turn out to be so bad on reverse hedges if your objectives are realized. Since you hope to purchase the warrants, which you previously sold short, at a few cents at expiration, the tax should be negligible. Of course you must pay the tax on the purchase of the optioned stock, unless it has been previously paid.

WHEN TO ACT

In order to take advantage of reverse hedge possibilities every listed warrant with less than three years to go before expiration should be under surveillance. After that the decision to act is almost mechanical. If the candidate meets the criteria set forth in this chapter and the potential profit percentage is better than you can obtain in an alternative position and you have the speculative funds, then invest. The decision to enter into the position is quite easy. Remember, however, that most exchanges ban short sales in expiring warrants when they have about three to six months to go or the short position becomes significant. Although the major exchanges claim not to have a hard rule of thumb, experience suggests that short sales are banned when the short position reaches between 20 percent and 30 percent of the total number listed. Canadian exchanges are more liberal in this area.

Many people claim that the decision to buy a security is easy, but complain that they just do not know when to sell. Getting in at the bottom and out at the top is an ideal that is seldom if ever achieved. Fortunately the very nature of the reverse hedge simplifies the getting out decision. Once the position has been entered it should be monitored from two points of view. First, if the position goes against you, it is time to get out. Knowing the breakeven points at expiration, it is easy to determine the stock price above and below which a loss develops. On the day you enter a position you should give your broker stops on both sides. A stop loss order is one wherein you specify a closeout price in anticipation of possible price movement. It is designed to limit your exposure. Some warrant traders try to salvage a reverse hedge position that has gone against them by adding to the long or short position to compensate for price movement. For most people this merely compounds the problem. Any decision to do so should be based on the same breakeven theory (probable and maximum profit analysis) as was used to enter the original position. In other words, the decision to modify an existing reverse hedge position is a decision to enter into a new one with different overall risks and probable rewards.

As experience and the usually low downside breakeven point (Point *A*) suggest, the losses that do develop are usually on the upside. Here the exposure to loss can be high except for those with almost unlimited funds. Using a diagram, such as Figure 7–3, or a table, such as the Appendix, it is easy to select the percent loss you are willing to absorb and then read off the corresponding stock price. Of course these percentages assume that the warrant sells at intrinsic value, which it probably will not do until expiration. In fact, with a rising stock price the premium may increase even though expiration is getting closer. The stop loss order price should be set in light of the current premium, assuming that it will be at least maintained on the upside.

Assuming that you are not stopped out over the life of the position, you are left with the pleasant task of deciding when to take your profits. Some warrant traders like to wait until shortly before expiration, especially if the stock sells significantly below the final exercise price, in order to eke out the last ounce of profit and satisfaction. However, this is not always the wisest decision. First, one sensible rule is to close out all reverse hedge positions at least six weeks before expiration. There are a number of reasons why this is a good rule of thumb. Most listed warrants are delisted a few days before expiration. You are much better off dealing on the exchange than you are OTC. All major exchanges announce well in advance the last trading day for an expiring warrant. Your broker should be told to notify you of this date. If the issuer is going to take any steps (such as extending the life of the warrant), then this is usually done during the last month of life. Since extending a warrant's life almost always results in a jump in the warrant's price, it is detrimental to those short. This is more fully discussed below. The most important consideration in deciding when to close a successful reverse hedge is the profits to be made by closing the position weighed against the profit to be gained by waiting longer. Some expiring warrants have lost most of their premium when they still have six or more weeks to go. On an annualized profit basis it may just not be worthwhile to stay in. Suppose you entered a reverse hedge at a three-to-one ratio with the stock at $7 and the warrant at $2 with a final per share exercise price of $15. Suppose the warrant now sells for 13 cents with the stock at $5. If the warrant has six weeks to go, how much additional profit can be made on the short side? Assuming that the stock remains the same, the answer is almost none. Even if the warrant hit zero, the potential profit on the short side is only 6.4 percent more than the current level ($2.00 versus $1.88). There is only one valid way to make a decision. You must weigh the probable profit of staying in the position versus that of getting out and investing in the best alternative reverse hedge available. Therefore the mechanics are easy. You assume that you close and immediately reopen the position. By mentally closing the position you can calculate that profit. Now you must determine the annualized probable profits to be gained by going right back in at the same ratio. If this is higher than the probable profits in other alternatives open to you, then you should stay in the original position. If the probable profits of reopening the same position are poor, then it is time to close the original position. If your analysis suggests that you might do well if you reentered the original position, but at a higher ratio, then it is probably worthwhile to short some additional warrants without any additional hedge. Therefore, part of the monitoring process on the downside involves an analysis of how the risk has changed. If a lower stock price at a date closer to expiration makes you feel that a higher ratio of warrants short to stock long is in order, you may be right. This new short position should be evaluated on its own merits (are there really any significant annualized profits to be made?) as well as with respect to the present position in the area of changed risk exposure.

POTENTIAL PITFALLS

Since the potential profits in reverse hedge positions are so high, it is logical to ask what can go wrong. There are a few potential pitfalls, but the probability of one occurring is exceedingly low.

One obvious problem creator is the extension of a warrant. If the issuer extends a warrant's life it is equivalent to issuing a new one and, in all probability, results in a significant jump in the warrant's price, especially if it is close (less than a year) to expiration. The legal aspects of a firm's extending the life of a warrant are unclear. Some warrant agreements stipulate that the life can be extended, in which case there is no problem. However, there has not been a court test on behalf of someone injured by an extension of a previously agreed upon expiration date. Fortunately, there have been only a few extensions in the last 10 years and these occurrences have been restricted to the smaller, OTC issues. The reasons for such a corporate action are clear. It is only for the benefit of insiders and others friendly to the issuer who also own a lot of warrants that such action is taken. A new breath of life for an otherwise worthless warrant is given as a favor. The action is clearly not in the interests of shareholders, assuming the exercise price is below the market price of the optioned stock, since in so extending, the issuer is agreeing to sell stock at a discount to warrantholders for longer than required by current warrant terms.

It is easy to avoid such a problem. Deal in listed warrants only and close out your reverse hedge at least six weeks before scheduled expiration. Most extensions are announced in the last few weeks of warrant life. Many exchanges, as a condition to listing a warrant, get company agreement that an extension or reduction in exercise price will not be effected, no matter what the warrant agreement says. In any case these things just do not happen with listed warrants.

Another pitfall that warrant traders worry about is the *short squeeze*. A short squeeze develops when a group of investors is able to buy essentially the entire floating supply of an issue and then force those short to buy back at its price. This happens more frequently in stocks than in warrants. The process of buying up the floating supply is commonly called *cornering the market*. This tactic is now outlawed by the major exchanges. The SEC is also on the watch for such unsavory tactics. Since the exchanges ban further short selling when the short position reaches a critical level, like 25 percent of the total issue outstanding, there is an exchange guarantee of an adequate supply. By following the simple rule of dealing in listed warrants with at least 100,000 outstanding, you should safely avoid squeezes. The statistics suggest that they are so infrequent and mild as to be just not worth worrying about. The most famous example is that of the Molybdenum warrant short squeeze of 1962, when a major corporation (International Mining) saw fit to accumulate the warrants. However, just before expiration the warrants dropped to essentially intrinsic value as a huge supply inundated the market. In those few cases where a corner has developed, those short were able to cover at favorable prices a few days before expiration. Only those who bought in early played into the hands of the manipulators. Manipulation of exchange-listed securities is for all practical purposes a thing of the past.

WARRANTS ON THE LONG SIDE

There is no way to recommend, except on an individual basis, the percentage of a fund that should be in warrants. For some it would be zero; for a few, 100 percent; and for most somewhere between 10 and 50 percent. People buy warrants because:

1. They believe in the stock market as a vehicle for long-term capital appreciation.
2. They believe in the sound prospects of the warrant's optioned stock.
3. They believe so strongly in the optioned stock that they are willing to assume what is usually an added risk in the warrant to obtain its leverage.

Following this logic it is easy to see how the investment decision is reached. All you need to do is determine how much risk you are willing to take for a potential reward. If you are absolutely sure about a stock, then it should never be purchased in lieu of the warrant. In fact, on absolute certainty, a call option is probably a better investment than the warrant. Unfortunately most of us do not deal with perfect information and must invest in the face of risk. In fact, the publication of figures on insider trading (officers', directors', and major shareholders') suggests that in many cases even those on the inside do not really know what is happening.

On the long side, warrants offer an opportunity for capital

gains that cannot be obtained as a rule in the optioned stock. If it is technically well situated and you are confident of the optioned stock, it is a buy.

As previously discussed, the risk inherent in a long warrant position can sometimes be reduced by shorting the optioned stock, creating a warrant hedge. This is a technique that again justifies the warrant's place in a number of portfolios, including some of the more conservative ones.

THE CASE FOR REVERSE HEDGES

Since 1966 the stock market, as measured by the popular averages, has managed to go nowhere as evidenced in Figure 7–10.

There is no guarantee that this will not continue. Such a market over a period of years makes successful investing a tough job. Such markets are characterized as being *whipsaw*, that is, investors are whipsawed in and out of the market by minor adjustments and never are able to enjoy a nice long ride. The reverse hedge is a technique that operates best in do-nothing markets. Since upon entering a reverse hedge you hope that the stock is at the exercise price (but will be perfectly happy if it is right where it is now) upon expiration many months hence, a stable market facilitates your operation.

One common frustration that bedevils most investors is their inability to make an immediate fortune in the market. In fact many investors work as long as 60 hours a week at their regular occupations to make a living, but hope to equal or surpass that income by spending at best a couple of hours a week studying the market and investing limited funds. When they fail to become new Bernard Baruchs they curse themselves and their brokers. In a sense, dealing in the stock

FIGURE 7–10
Dow Jones Industrial Average

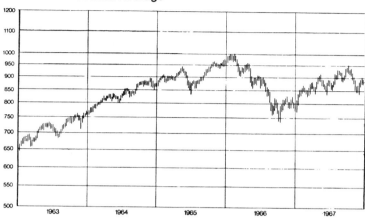

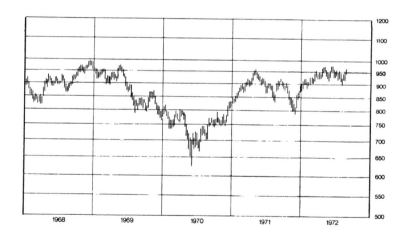

market is not unlike farming; you reap what you sow. Hard work may produce results. However, there are no guarantees. Again, the reverse hedge is a technique that lends itself to use by people who have jobs other than that of security analyst. The use of the technique is based on a technical evaluation of the warrant-stock relationship rather than a fundamental analysis. This makes the job easier, less risky, and less time-consuming.

WHAT IS FORTUNE

One man's definition of a fortune is another's description of abject poverty. It is all relative. However, the word *millionaire* has had a significant meaning to men everywhere for decades. It does not matter if the specie is dollars, pounds, francs, or whatever, the object is to acquire one million of them. In England, with a current exchange rate of $2.40 to the pound, this makes the job 240 percent tougher. And yet the concept of millionaire exists in England, and it means one million pounds. People labor all over the world to reach the magic number.

Reaching the level of $1 million in net worth should be an easy task, some claim, in the United States of America. In and around New York City the job becomes quite easy, since there are a number of social functions where you can find a surplus of Wall Streeters or their friends. When the market is booming (or getting ready to do so, which is anytime) you can find at least one person at almost any social gathering who has a stock that is to double in the next few weeks. The credence you place in this person's story is based on the two or three stocks he or she has already had this year which have doubled. Now a little calculation is in order. How many social functions must you attend to become a millionaire? Starting with a mere $1,000, doubling it 10 times, you will end up with $1,024,000 before taxes. Not bad. All that is required is that you attend 10 parties, pick up 10 tips, play them, and collect $1 million. It sounds easy; just pick 10 in a row. However, some other facts are quite sobering.

How many millionaires do you think there are in the United States? It may be quite surprising to find that out of over 200 million people there are only about 100,000 bona fide millionaires, or 0.05 percent. This number is more significant when you discover that most of these fortunes were not made in the stock market, but were inherited. The major fortunes now held in the United States were made in such areas as railroads, oil, cattle, and banking during the great business expansion of the country (1870 through 1930) when taxes were almost nonexistent. Although these facts may not put a dent in your ambition to make $1 million, they should make you feel better if you end up with half a loaf.

The accumulation of a few hundred thousand dollars over a number of years is an attainable goal for the astute investor. The power of compound interest and the techniques of the reverse hedge are the keys.

ATTAINABLE FORTUNES

The power of compound interest is quite interesting. As Figure 7–11 demonstrates, it is possible for a small sum, such as $1,000, to grow into something worthwhile over time.

As an example, if you invested $1,000 now and it grew at 20 percent per year, you would have $237,380 in 30 years. If it grew at 30 percent, then the accumulated value would be $2,620,000 in 30 years or $190,000 in 20 years. This table may be used for other starting values. If $5,000 is invested now and it grows at 30 percent, then it will accumulate to $255,830 (5 times 51,186) in just 15 years. Similarly, $10,000 invested now and growing at 20 percent yields $383,380 in 20 years. The table should be useful for your own planning.

There is another method of planning for the accumulation

FIGURE 7-11
Amount to Which $1,000 Will Grow at Indicated Growth Rate

Years	6%	8%	10%	15%	20%	24%	30%	40%	50%
1	$1,060	$1,080	$1,100	$1,150	$1,200	$1,240	$1,300	$1,400	$1,500
2	1,124	1,166	1,210	1,323	1,440	1,538	1,690	1,960	2,250
3	1,191	1,260	1,331	1,521	1,728	1,907	2,197	2,744	3,375
4	1,263	1,361	1,464	1,750	2,074	2,364	2,856	3,842	5,063
5	1,338	1,494	1,611	2,011	2,488	2,932	3,713	5,378	7,594
6	1,419	1,587	1,772	2,313	2,986	3,635	4,827	7,530	11,391
7	1,504	1,714	1,949	2,660	3,583	4,508	6,275	10,541	17,086
8	1,594	1,851	2,144	3,059	4,300	5,590	8,157	14,758	25,629
9	1,690	1,999	2,358	3,518	5,160	6,931	10,604	20,661	38,443
10	1,791	2,159	2,594	4,046	6,192	8,595	13,786	28,925	57,665
11	1,898	2,332	2,853	4,652	7,430	10,658	17,922	40,496	86,498
12	2,012	2,518	3,138	5,350	8,916	13,215	23,298	56,694	129,750
13	2,133	2,720	3,452	6,153	10,700	16,386	30,288	79,371	194,620
14	2,261	2,937	3,798	7,076	12,839	20,319	39,374	111,120	291,930
15	2,397	3,172	4,177	8,137	15,407	25,196	51,186	165,570	437,890
16	2,540	3,426	4,595	9,358	18,488	31,243	66,542	217,800	656,840
17	2,693	3,700	5,055	10,761	22,186	38,741	86,504	304,910	985,260
18	2,854	3,997	5,560	12,375	26,623	48,039	112,460	426,880	1,477,900
19	3,026	4,316	6,116	14,232	31,948	59,568	146,190	597,630	2,216,800
20	3,207	4,661	6,728	16,367	38,338	73,864	190,050	836,688	3,325,300
25	4,292	6,849	10,835	32,919	95,396	216,540	705,640	4,499,900	25,251,000
30	5,744	10,063	17,449	66,212	237,380	634,820	2,620,000	24,201,000	191,750,000

of capital. Instead of starting with a fixed sum, as above, a specific dollar amount is invested on a regular basis, such as monthly or quarterly. Figure 7–12 shows how such a program would operate at various growth rates assuming $1,000 is invested each year.

The numbers shown assume that this $1,000 is evenly invested, such as $83 per month. However, as long as the infusion is $1,000 per year and it takes place on average in the middle of the year, the numbers are quite accurate. If the sum is in on average by May, then the results would be slightly better; if in July, slightly worse. Here $1,000 invested every year for 20 years grows to $204,790 at 20 percent or $720,560 at 30 percent. If $2,000 per year were invested, then these numbers double. Again the table is useful for your own planning at other rates and periods of time.

Of course the next question is what can you expect as an attainable rate of growth. Savings accounts and other cash equivalents (Treasury Bills) may do 6 percent or so. As the tables suggest, there is not much hope of accumulating wealth at this rate unless a lot of your own capital is ploughed in. Figure 7–8 suggests that it might be possible to do about 69 percent per year in the reverse hedge game. Others feel happy to do 15 percent per year in basically long securities positions. Using the tools in this book and those skills you have acquired elsewhere you must set a personal growth objective and amount of money to be committed to the effort. For the professional warrant trader a 30 percent growth rate in the total portfolio is not unreasonable. For the average mutual fund 10 percent is good. However, those conversant with hedging and reverse hedging in warrants should be able to do 20 to 30 percent per year, assuming a stable market. By investing $5,000 now or $1,000 per year for 20 years, a couple hundred thousand dollars can be accumulated at 20

FIGURE 7-12
Amount to Which $1,000 Per Year Invested Evenly during the Year Will Grow at Indicated Rate

Years	6%	8%	10%	15%	20%	24%	30%
1	$ 1,030	$ 1,040	$ 1,049	$ 1,073	$ 1,097	$ 1,116	$ 1,143
2	2,121	2,162	2,203	2,308	2,413	2,500	2,630
3	3,278	3,375	3,473	3,726	3,993	4,215	4,562
4	4,505	4,684	4,869	5,359	5,889	6,342	7,075
5	5,805	6,098	6,406	7,236	8,163	8,980	10,340
6	7,183	7,625	8,095	9,395	10,893	12,250	14,586
7	8,643	9,275	9,954	11,877	14,168	16,306	20,105
8	10,192	11,057	11,999	14,732	18,099	21,335	27,280
9	11,833	12,981	14,248	18,015	22,816	27,572	36,607
10	13,572	15,059	16,722	21,791	28,476	35,305	48,733
11	15,416	17,303	19,443	26,133	35,268	44,893	64,497
12	17,371	19,726	22,437	31,126	43,418	56,784	84,989
13	19,443	22,344	25,729	36,868	53,199	71,527	111,630
14	21,639	25,171	29,352	43,472	64,936	89,810	146,260
15	23,967	28,224	33,336	51,066	79,020	112,480	191,280
16	26,435	31,522	37,719	59,799	95,921	140,590	249,810
17	29,051	35,083	42,540	69,842	116,200	175,450	325,900
18	31,824	38,929	47,843	81,392	140,540	218,670	424,810
19	34,763	43,083	53,676	94,674	169,740	272,270	553,400
20	37,878	47,569	60,093	109,950	204,790	338,730	720,560
25	56,494	75,993	103,190	228,380	517,750	1,002,000	2,685,700
30	81,407	117,760	172,590	466,590	1,296,500	2,946,500	9,982,300

percent and well over a half million dollars at 30 percent. Even with taxes considered, the net amount left is a tidy sum. As suggested by the tables, it is not so important to start with large sums of money as it is to start early. In as little as 10 or 15 years it is possible to accumulate some wealth with a modest investment. However, in 20 or more years it is far easier as growth compounds on larger capital bases.

The key to success is to be found in the development of a personal plan and commitment. If these are present, then in the long run diversification in warrant investments has a good chance to pay off.

Appendix

T HIS IS AN ANALYSIS of the warrants that qualified as reverse hedge candidates on July 30, 1971, under the selection rules given in Chapter 7. At that time margin requirements were 65 percent in the United States.

KEY TO APPENDIX

The items on each page, reading left to right for the two
rows of headings, are:

Item	*Use*
Optioned Stock Name	Name of company.
"Wt Exch"	Exchange where warrant trades, abbreviations are same as those in Figure 7–5.

"Mo to Exp"	Months to expiration date as of July 30, 1971.
"Final Exc Pr"	Final per share exercise price.
"Stock"	Stock price as of July 30, 1971.
"S/E Fnl"	Stock price divided by final per share exercise price.
"Warrant"	Warrant price as of July 30, 1971.
"Ratio"	Reverse hedge ratio of warrants short to shares long.
"R"	Effective ratio based on number of shares called by each warrant.
"A"	Stock price below which a loss develops at specified ratio.
"PC"	The percentage by which the stock can decrease before a loss develops for the specified ratio.
"PC/Mo"	The percentage per month by which the stock can decrease before a loss develops for the specified ratio.
"Max at"	Stock price or range that affords the maximum profit at the indicated ratio. "E" is the per share exercise price.
"B"	Stock price above which a loss develops at specified ratio.
"PC"	The percentage by which the stock can increase before a loss develops for a specified ratio.
"PC/Mo"	The percentage per month by which the stock can increase

	before a loss develops for the specified ratio.
"Bare Acct Invest"	The investment required to support the investment suggested by the specified ratio and prices using the margin requirements applicable on July 30, 1971.
"Maximum Profit Act"	The maximum actual profit percentage assuming stock is at price suggested in "Max at" column upon warrant expiration.
"Maximum Profit Ann"	The maximum actual profit expressed as an annualized percentage.
"Probable Profit Act"	The probable actual profit percentage assuming stock is at current price upon warrant expiration.
"Probable Profit Ann"	The probable actual profit percentage expressed as an annualized percentage.

Reverse Hedge Analysis (July 30, 1971)

ATLANTIC RICHFIELD	WT EXCH	MO TO EXP	FINAL EXC PR	STOCK	S/E FNL	WARRANT
	ASE	13.1	$110.00	$65.50	.60	$ 4.13

RATIO	R	A	PC	PC/MO	MAX AT	B	PC	PC/MO	BARE ACCT INVEST	MAXIMUM PROFIT		PROBABLE PROFIT	
										ACT	ANN	ACT	ANN
1/1	1.0000	$61.37	- 6	+0	E+	$999.99	+999	+999	$65.50	74	68	6	6
2/1	2.0000	$57.24	-13	-1	E	$162.76	+148	+ 11	$65.50	81	74	13	12
3/1	3.0000	$53.11	-19	-1	E	$138.45	+111	+ 9	$65.50	87	80	19	17
4/1	4.0000	$48.98	-25	-2	E	$130.34	+ 99	+ 8	$65.50	93	86	25	23
5/1	5.0000	$44.85	-32	-2	E	$126.29	+ 93	+ 7	$65.50	99	91	32	29
6/1	6.0000	$40.72	-38	-3	E	$123.86	+ 89	+ 7	$67.36	103	95	37	34
7/1	7.0000	$36.59	-44	-3	E	$122.24	+ 87	+ 7	$71.49	103	95	40	37
8/1	8.0000	$32.46	-50	-4	E	$121.08	+ 85	+ 7	$75.62	103	95	44	40
9/1	9.0000	$28.33	-57	-4	E	$120.21	+ 84	+ 6	$79.75	102	94	47	43
SHORT					0-E	$114.13	+ 74	+ 6	$ 4.13	100	92	100	92

	WT EXCH	MO TO EXP	FINAL EXC PR	STOCK	S/E FNL	WARRANT
AVCO COMMUNITY DEVELOPERS	PC	28.6	$ 6.50	$ 5.00	.77	$ 2.88

RATIO	R	A	PC	PC/MO	MAX AT	B	PC	PC/MO	BARE ACCT INVEST	MAXIMUM PROFIT ACT	MAXIMUM PROFIT ANN	PROBABLE PROFIT ACT	PROBABLE PROFIT ANN
1/1	1.0000	$ 2.12	- 58	-2	E+	$999.99	+999	+999	$ 6.13	71	30	47	20
2/1	2.0000	$ .76-	-100	-4	E	$ 13.76	+175	+ 6	$ 9.01	81	34	64	27
3/1	3.0000	$ 3.64-	-100	-4	E	$ 11.57	+131	+ 5	$11.89	85	36	73	31
4/1	4.0000	$ 6.52-	-100	-4	E	$ 10.84	+117	+ 4	$14.77	88	37	78	33
5/1	5.0000	$ 9.40-	-100	-4	E	$ 10.48	+110	+ 4	$17.65	90	38	82	34
6/1	6.0000	$12.28-	-100	-4	E	$ 10.26	+105	+ 4	$20.53	91	38	84	35
7/1	7.0000	$15.16-	-100	-4	E	$ 10.11	+102	+ 4	$23.41	93	39	86	36
8/1	8.0000	$18.04-	-100	-4	E	$ 10.01	+100	+ 4	$26.29	93	39	88	37
9/1	9.0000	$20.92-	-100	-4	E	$ 9.93	+ 99	+ 3	$29.17	94	40	89	37
SHORT					0-E	$ 9.38	+ 88	+ 3	$ 2.88	100	42	100	42

BLUEBIRD

	WT EXCH	MO TO EXP	FINAL EXC PR	STOCK	S/E FNL	WARRANT
	ASE	32.3	$ 10.75	$ 6.38	.59	$ 3.13

RATIO	R	A	PC	PC/MO	MAX AT	B	PC	PC/MO	BARE ACCT INVEST	MAXIMUM PROFIT ACT	MAXIMUM PROFIT ANN	PROBABLE PROFIT ACT	PROBABLE PROFIT ANN
1/1	1.0000	$ 3.25	− 49	−2	E+	$999.99	+999	+999	$ 7.28	103	38	43	16
2/1	2.0000	$ .12	− 98	−3	E	$ 21.38	+235	+ 7	$10.41	102	38	60	22
3/1	3.0000	$ 3.01−	−100	−3	E	$ 17.63	+176	+ 5	$13.54	102	38	69	26
4/1	4.0000	$ 6.14−	−100	−3	E	$ 16.38	+157	+ 5	$16.67	101	38	75	28
5/1	5.0000	$ 9.27−	−100	−3	E	$ 15.76	+147	+ 5	$19.80	101	38	79	29
6/1	6.0000	$12.40−	−100	−3	E	$ 15.38	+141	+ 4	$22.93	101	38	82	30
7/1	7.0000	$15.53−	−100	−3	E	$ 15.13	+137	+ 4	$26.06	101	38	84	31
8/1	8.0000	$18.66−	−100	−3	E	$ 14.95	+134	+ 4	$29.19	101	38	86	32
9/1	9.0000	$21.79−	−100	−3	E	$ 14.82	+132	+ 4	$32.32	101	38	87	32
SHORT					0−E	$ 13.88	+118	+ 4	$ 3.13	100	37	100	37

CANADA SOUTHERN PETE

	WT EXCH	MO TO EXP	FINAL EXC PR	S/E FNL	WARRANT
	TOR	29.0	$ 5.75	.98	$ 2.95
			STOCK		
			$ 5.65		

RATIO	R	A	PC	PC/MO	MAX AT	FINAL EXC PR B	STOCK PC	PC/MO	BARE ACCT INVEST	MAXIMUM PROFIT ACT	MAXIMUM PROFIT ANN	PROBABLE PROFIT ACT	PROBABLE PROFIT ANN
1/1	1.0000	$ 2.70	- 52	-2	E+	$999.99	+999	+999	$ 5.65	54	22	52	21
2/1	2.0000	$ .25–	–100	–3	E	$ 11.75	+108	+ 4	$ 5.79	104	43	102	42
3/1	3.0000	$ 3.20–	–100	–3	E	$ 10.23	+ 81	+ 3	$ 7.27	123	51	122	50
4/1	4.0000	$ 6.15–	–100	–3	E	$ 9.72	+ 72	+ 2	$ 8.75	136	56	135	56
5/1	5.0000	$ 9.10–	–100	–3	E	$ 9.46	+ 67	+ 2	$10.23	145	60	144	60
6/1	6.0000	$12.05–	–100	–3	E	$ 9.31	+ 65	+ 2	$11.71	152	63	151	62
7/1	7.0000	$15.00–	–100	–3	E	$ 9.21	+ 63	+ 2	$13.19	157	65	157	65
8/1	8.0000	$17.95–	–100	–3	E	$ 9.14	+ 62	+ 2	$14.67	162	67	161	67
9/1	9.0000	$20.90–	–100	–3	E	$ 9.08	+ 61	+ 2	$16.15	165	68	164	68
SHORT					0–E	$ 8.70	+ 54	+ 2	$ 1.48	199	82	199	82

	WT EXCH	MO TO EXP	FINAL EXC PR	STOCK	S/E FNL	WARRANT
	ASE	27.5	$ 20.60	$ 6.25	.30	$ 1.63

ELGIN NATIONAL INDUSTRIES

RATIO	R	A	PC	PC/MO	MAX AT	B	PC	PC/MO	BARE ACCT INVEST	MAXIMUM PROFIT ACT	MAXIMUM PROFIT ANN	PROBABLE PROFIT ACT	PROBABLE PROFIT ANN
3/1	1.2000	$ 1.36	- 78	-3	E	$116.80	+999	+999	$11.56	166	72	42	18
4/1	1.6000	$ .27-	-100	-4	E	$ 55.38	+786	+ 29	$14.06	148	65	46	20
5/1	2.0000	$ 1.90-	-100	-4	E	$ 43.10	+590	+ 21	$16.56	136	59	49	21
6/1	2.4000	$ 3.53-	-100	-4	E	$ 37.84	+505	+ 18	$19.06	127	55	51	22
7/1	2.8000	$ 5.16-	-100	-4	E	$ 34.91	+459	+ 17	$21.56	119	52	53	23
8/1	3.2000	$ 6.79-	-100	-4	E	$ 33.05	+429	+ 16	$24.06	114	50	54	24
9/1	3.6000	$ 8.42-	-100	-4	E	$ 31.76	+408	+ 15	$26.56	109	48	55	24
10/1	4.0000	$10.05-	-100	-4	E	$ 30.82	+393	+ 14	$29.06	105	46	56	24
11/1	4.4000	$11.68-	-100	-4	E	$ 30.09	+381	+ 14	$31.56	102	44	57	25
12/1	4.8000	$13.31-	-100	-4	E	$ 29.52	+372	+ 14	$34.06	100	44	57	25
13/1	5.2000	$14.94-	-100	-4	E	$ 29.06	+365	+ 13	$36.56	97	42	58	25
14/1	5.6000	$16.57-	-100	-4	E	$ 28.68	+359	+ 13	$39.06	95	41	58	25
15/1	6.0000	$18.20-	-100	-4	E	$ 28.36	+354	+ 13	$41.56	93	41	59	26
16/1	6.4000	$19.83-	-100	-4	E	$ 28.09	+349	+ 13	$44.06	92	40	59	26
17/1	6.8000	$21.46-	-100	-4	E	$ 27.85	+346	+ 13	$46.56	90	39	60	26
18/1	7.2000	$23.09-	-100	-4	E	$ 27.65	+342	+ 12	$49.06	89	39	60	26
19/1	7.6000	$24.72-	-100	-4	E	$ 27.47	+340	+ 12	$51.56	88	38	60	26
20/1	8.0000	$26.35-	-100	-4	E	$ 27.31	+337	+ 12	$54.06	87	38	60	26
21/1	8.4000	$27.98-	-100	-4	E	$ 27.16	+335	+ 12	$56.56	86	38	61	27
22/1	8.8000	$29.61-	-100	-4	E	$ 27.04	+333	+ 12	$59.06	85	37	61	27
23/1	9.2000	$31.24-	-100	-4	E	$ 26.92	+331	+ 12	$61.56	84	37	61	27
SHORT					0-E	$ 24.68	+295	+ 11	$ 2.50	65	28	65	28

		WT EXCH	MO TO EXP	FINAL EXC PR	STOCK	S/E FNL	WARRANT
GAZ METROPOLITAIN '63		TOR	22.1	$ 6.00	$ 5.75	.96	$ 2.17

RATIO	R	A	PC	PC/MO	MAX AT	B	PC	PC/MO	BARE ACCT INVEST	MAXIMUM PROFIT		PROBABLE PROFIT	
										ACT	ANN	ACT	ANN
1/1	1.0000	$ 3.58	− 38	−2	E+	$999.99	+999	+999	$ 5.75	42	23	38	21
2/1	2.0000	$ 1.41	− 75	−3	E	$ 10.59	+ 84	+ 4	$ 5.75	80	44	75	41
3/1	3.0000	$ .76−	−100	−5	E	$ 9.38	+ 63	+ 3	$ 6.15	110	60	106	58
4/1	4.0000	$ 2.93−	−100	−5	E	$ 8.98	+ 56	+ 3	$ 7.24	123	67	120	65
5/1	5.0000	$ 5.10−	−100	−5	E	$ 8.78	+ 53	+ 2	$ 8.33	133	72	130	71
6/1	6.0000	$ 7.27−	−100	−5	E	$ 8.65	+ 50	+ 2	$ 9.42	141	77	138	75
7/1	7.0000	$ 9.44−	−100	−5	E	$ 8.57	+ 49	+ 2	$10.51	147	80	145	79
8/1	8.0000	$11.61−	−100	−5	E	$ 8.52	+ 48	+ 2	$11.60	152	83	150	82
9/1	9.0000	$13.78−	−100	−5	E	$ 8.47	+ 47	+ 2	$12.69	156	85	154	84
SHORT					0−E	$ 8.17	+ 42	+ 2	$ 1.09	199	108	199	108

HOUSTON OILS LTD

WT EXCH	TOR		
MO TO EXP	16.5		
FINAL EXC PR	$ 3.50		
STOCK	$ 2.37		
S/E FNL	.68		
WARRANT	$ 1.11		

RATIO	R	A	PC	PC/MO	MAX AT	B	PC	PC/MO	BARE ACCT INVEST	MAXIMUM PROFIT		PROBABLE PROFIT	
										ACT	ANN	ACT	ANN
1/1	1.0000	$1.26	- 47	-3	E+	$999.99	+999	+999	$ 2.37	95	69	47	34
2/1	2.0000	$ .15	- 94	-6	E	$ 6.85	+189	+ 11	$ 3.41	98	71	65	47
3/1	3.0000	$ .96-	-100	-6	E	$ 5.73	+142	+ 9	$ 4.52	99	72	74	54
4/1	4.0000	$2.07-	-100	-6	E	$ 5.36	+126	+ 8	$ 5.63	99	72	79	57
5/1	5.0000	$3.18-	-100	-6	E	$ 5.17	+118	+ 7	$ 6.74	99	72	82	60
6/1	6.0000	$4.29-	-100	-6	E	$ 5.06	+114	+ 7	$ 7.85	99	72	85	62
7/1	7.0000	$5.40-	-100	-6	E	$ 4.98	+110	+ 7	$ 8.96	99	72	87	63
8/1	8.0000	$6.51-	-100	-6	E	$ 4.93	+108	+ 7	$10.07	99	72	88	64
9/1	9.0000	$7.62-	-100	-6	E	$ 4.89	+106	+ 6	$11.18	99	72	89	65
SHORT					0-E	$ 4.61	+ 95	+ 6	$ 1.11	100	73	100	73

HUSKY OIL LTD

	WT EXCH	MOTO EXP	FINAL EXC PR	STOCK	S/E FNL	WARRANT
	TOR	35.0	$ 16.50	$ 16.38	.99	$ 7.35

RATIO	R	A	PC	PC/MO	MAX AT	B	PC	PC/MO	BARE ACCT INVEST	MAXIMUM PROFIT ACT	MAXIMUM PROFIT ANN	PROBABLE PROFIT ACT	PROBABLE PROFIT ANN
1/1	1.0000	$ 9.03	− 45	−1	E+	$999.99	+999	+999	$16.38	46	16	45	15
2/1	2.0000	$ 1.68	− 90	−3	E	$ 31.32	+ 91	+ 3	$16.38	90	31	90	31
3/1	3.0000	$ 5.67−	−100	−3	E	$ 27.59	+ 68	+ 2	$19.23	115	39	115	39
4/1	4.0000	$13.02−	−100	−3	E	$ 26.34	+ 61	+ 2	$22.91	129	44	128	44
5/1	5.0000	$20.37−	−100	−3	E	$ 25.72	+ 57	+ 2	$26.59	139	48	138	47
6/1	6.0000	$27.72−	−100	−3	E	$ 25.34	+ 55	+ 2	$30.27	146	50	146	50
7/1	7.0000	$35.07−	−100	−3	E	$ 25.10	+ 53	+ 2	$33.95	152	52	152	52
8/1	8.0000	$42.42−	−100	−3	E	$ 24.92	+ 52	+ 1	$37.63	157	54	156	53
9/1	9.0000	$49.77−	−100	−3	E	$ 24.78	+ 51	+ 1	$41.31	160	55	160	55
SHORT					0−E	$ 23.85	+ 46	+ 1	$ 3.68	200	69	200	69

LECTRO MANAGEMENT

	WT EXCH	MO TO EXP	FINAL EXC PR	STOCK	S/E FNL	WARRANT
	NTL	10.0	$ 8.80	$ 2.50	.28	$ .75

RATIO	R	A	PC	PC/MO	MAX AT	B	PC	PC/MO	BARE ACCT INVEST	MAXIMUM PROFIT		PROBABLE PROFIT	
										ACT	ANN	ACT	ANN
1/1	1.0000	$1.75	− 30	− 3	E+	$999.99	+999	+999	$ 4.13	171	205	18	22
2/1	2.0000	$1.00	− 60	− 6	E	$ 16.60	+564	+ 56	$ 6.63	118	141	23	28
3/1	3.0000	$ .25	− 90	− 9	E	$ 13.08	+423	+ 42	$ 9.13	94	112	25	30
4/1	4.0000	$ .50−	−100	−10	E	$ 11.90	+376	+ 37	$11.63	80	96	26	31
5/1	5.0000	$1.25−	−100	−10	E	$ 11.31	+352	+ 35	$14.13	71	85	27	32
6/1	6.0000	$2.00−	−100	−10	E	$ 10.96	+338	+ 34	$16.63	65	78	27	32
7/1	7.0000	$2.75−	−100	−10	E	$ 10.73	+329	+ 33	$19.13	60	72	27	32
8/1	8.0000	$3.50−	−100	−10	E	$ 10.56	+322	+ 32	$21.63	57	68	28	33
9/1	9.0000	$4.25−	−100	−10	E	$ 10.43	+317	+ 32	$24.13	54	65	28	33
SHORT					0−E	$ 9.55	+282	+ 28	$ 2.50	30	36	30	36

MAGELLAN PETROLEUM

	WT EXCH	MO TO EXP	FINAL EXC PR	S/E FNL	WARRANT	STOCK
	PC	5.0	$ 5.25	.79	$ 1.00	$ 4.13

RATIO	R	A	PC	PC/MO	MAX AT	FINAL EXC PR B	STOCK PC	PC/MO	BARE ACCT INVEST	MAXIMUM PROFIT ACT	MAXIMUM PROFIT ANN	PROBABLE PROFIT ACT	PROBABLE PROFIT ANN
1/1	1.0000	$3.13	- 24	- 5	E+	$999.99	+999	+999	$ 5.18	41	98	19	45
2/1	2.0000	$2.13	- 48	-10	E	$ 8.37	+103	+ 20	$ 7.68	41	98	26	62
3/1	3.0000	$1.13	- 73	-15	E	$ 7.31	+ 77	+ 15	$10.18	40	95	29	69
4/1	4.0000	$ .13	- 97	-19	E	$ 6.96	+ 69	+ 14	$12.68	40	95	32	76
5/1	5.0000	$ .87-	-100	-20	E	$ 6.78	+ 64	+ 13	$15.18	40	95	33	79
6/1	6.0000	$1.87-	-100	-20	E	$ 6.67	+ 62	+ 12	$17.68	40	95	34	81
7/1	7.0000	$2.87-	-100	-20	E	$ 6.60	+ 60	+ 12	$20.18	40	95	35	83
8/1	8.0000	$3.87-	-100	-20	E	$ 6.55	+ 59	+ 12	$22.68	40	95	35	83
9/1	9.0000	$4.87-	-100	-20	E	$ 6.52	+ 58	+ 12	$25.18	40	95	36	86
SHORT					0-E	$ 6.25	+ 51	+ 10	$ 2.50	40	95	40	95

MARKBOROUGH PROPERTIES

	WT EXCH	MO TO EXP	FINAL EXC PR	STOCK	S/E FNL	WARRANT
	TOR	12.1	$ 7.00	$ 5.00	.71	$ 1.05

RATIO	R	A	PC	PC/MO	MAX AT	B	PC	PC/MO	BARE ACCT INVEST	MAXIMUM PROFIT ACT	ANN	PROBABLE PROFIT ACT	ANN
1/1	1.0000	$3.95	− 21	−2	E+	$999.99	+999	+999	$ 5.00	61	61	21	21
2/1	2.0000	$2.90	− 42	−3	E	$ 11.10	+122	+ 10	$ 5.00	82	82	42	42
3/1	3.0000	$1.85	− 63	−5	E	$ 9.58	+ 92	+ 8	$ 5.65	91	91	56	56
4/1	4.0000	$ .80	− 84	−7	E	$ 9.07	+ 81	+ 7	$ 6.70	93	93	63	63
5/1	5.0000	$ .25−	−100	−8	E	$ 8.81	+ 76	+ 6	$ 7.75	94	94	68	68
6/1	6.0000	$1.30−	−100	−8	E	$ 8.66	+ 73	+ 6	$ 8.80	94	94	72	72
7/1	7.0000	$2.35−	−100	−8	E	$ 8.56	+ 71	+ 6	$ 9.85	95	95	75	75
8/1	8.0000	$3.40−	−100	−8	E	$ 8.49	+ 70	+ 6	$10.90	95	95	77	77
9/1	9.0000	$4.45−	−100	−8	E	$ 8.43	+ 69	+ 6	$11.95	96	96	79	79
SHORT					0−E	$ 8.05	+ 61	+ 5	$ 1.05	100	100	100	100

REPUBLIC MORTGAGE INVES‾

		WT EXCH	MO TO EXP	FINAL EXC PR	STOCK	S/E FNL	WARRANT
		ASE	35.0	$ 20.00	$ 19.25	.96	$ 5.13

RATIO	R	A	PC	PC/MO	MAX AT	FINAL EXC PR B	STOCK PC	PC/MO	BARE ACCT INVEST	MAXIMUM PROFIT ACT	MAXIMUM PROFIT ANN	PROBABLE PROFIT ACT	PROBABLE PROFIT ANN
1/1	1.0000	$14.12	- 27	-1	E+	$999.99	+999	+999	$19.25	31	11	27	9
2/1	2.0000	$ 8.99	- 53	-2	E	$ 31.01	+ 61	+ 2	$22.51	49	17	46	16
3/1	3.0000	$ 3.86	- 80	-2	E	$ 28.07	+ 46	+ 1	$27.51	59	20	56	19
4/1	4.0000	$ 1.27–	-100	-3	E	$ 27.09	+ 41	+ 1	$32.51	65	22	63	22
5/1	5.0000	$ 6.40–	-100	-3	E	$ 26.60	+ 38	+ 1	$37.51	70	24	68	23
6/1	6.0000	$11.53–	-100	-3	E	$ 26.31	+ 37	+ 1	$42.51	74	25	72	25
7/1	7.0000	$16.66–	-100	-3	E	$ 26.11	+ 36	+ 1	$47.51	77	26	76	26
8/1	8.0000	$21.79–	-100	-3	E	$ 25.97	+ 35	+ 1	$52.51	80	27	78	27
9/1	9.0000	$26.92–	-100	-3	E	$ 25.87	+ 34	+ 1	$57.51	82	28	80	27
SHORT					0–E	$ 25.13	+ 31	+ 1	$ 5.00	103	35	103	35

TEXAS INTERNATIONAL PETE

	WT EXCH	MO TO EXP	FINAL EXC PR	STOCK	S/E FNL	WARRANT
	PC	34.1	$ 9.00	$ 8.00	.89	$ 4.88

RATIO	R	A	PC	PC/MO	MAX AT	FINAL EXC PR B	STOCK PC	PC/MO	BARE ACCT INVEST	MAXIMUM PROFIT ACT	ANN	PROBABLE PROFIT ACT	ANN
1/1	1.0000	$ 3.12	− 61	−2	E+	$999.99	+999	+999	$10.08	58	20	48	17
2/1	2.0000	$ 1.76−	−100	−3	E	$ 19.76	+147	+ 4	$14.96	72	25	65	23
3/1	3.0000	$ 6.64−	−100	−3	E	$ 16.82	+110	+ 3	$19.84	79	28	74	26
4/1	4.0000	$11.52−	−100	−3	E	$ 15.84	+ 98	+ 3	$24.72	83	29	79	28
5/1	5.0000	$16.40−	−100	−3	E	$ 15.35	+ 92	+ 3	$29.60	86	30	82	29
6/1	6.0000	$21.28−	−100	−3	E	$ 15.06	+ 88	+ 3	$34.48	88	31	85	30
7/1	7.0000	$26.16−	−100	−3	E	$ 14.86	+ 86	+ 3	$39.36	89	31	87	31
8/1	8.0000	$31.04−	−100	−3	E	$ 14.72	+ 84	+ 2	$44.24	91	32	88	31
9/1	9.0000	$35.92−	−100	−3	E	$ 14.62	+ 83	+ 2	$49.12	91	32	89	31
SHORT					0−E	$ 13.88	+ 74	+ 2	$ 4.88	100	35	100	35

TRADERS GROUP A '65

		WT EXCH	MO TO EXP	FINAL EXC PR	STOCK	S/E FNL	WARRANT
		TOR	15.5	$ 15.00	$ 14.00	.93	$ 2.25

RATIO	R	A	PC	PC/MO	MAX AT	B	PC	PC/MO	BARE ACCT INVEST	MAXIMUM PROFIT ACT	MAXIMUM PROFIT ANN	PROBABLE PROFIT ACT	PROBABLE PROFIT ANN
1/1	1.0000	$11.75	– 16	–1	E+	$999.99	+999	+999	$14.00	23	18	16	12
2/1	2.0000	$ 9.50	– 32	–2	E	$ 20.50	+ 46	+ 3	$14.00	39	30	32	25
3/1	3.0000	$ 7.25	– 48	–3	E	$ 18.88	+ 35	+ 2	$14.00	55	43	48	37
4/1	4.0000	$ 5.00	– 64	–4	E	$ 18.33	+ 31	+ 2	$14.00	71	55	64	50
5/1	5.0000	$ 2.75	– 80	–5	E	$ 18.06	+ 29	+ 2	$14.00	88	68	80	62
6/1	6.0000	$ .50	– 96	–6	E	$ 17.90	+ 28	+ 2	$14.00	104	80	96	74
7/1	7.0000	$ 1.75–	–100	–6	E	$ 17.79	+ 27	+ 2	$14.91	112	87	106	82
8/1	8.0000	$ 4.00–	–100	–6	E	$ 17.71	+ 27	+ 2	$16.04	118	91	112	87
9/1	9.0000	$ 6.25–	–100	–6	E	$ 17.66	+ 26	+ 2	$17.17	124	96	118	91
SHORT					0–E	$ 17.25	+ 23	+ 1	$ 1.13	199	154	199	154

UNITED CANSO OIL & GAS

	WT EXCH	MO TO EXP	FINAL EXC PR	STOCK	S/E FNL	WARRANT
	TOR	8.0	$ 5.25	$ 5.20	.99	$ 1.83

RATIO	R	A	PC	PC/MO	MAX AT	B	PC	PC/MO	BARE ACCT INVEST	MAXIMUM PROFIT ACT	ANN	PROBABLE PROFIT ACT	ANN
1/1	1.0000	$ 3.37	- 35	- 4	E+	$999.99	+999	+999	$ 5.20	36	54	35	53
2/1	2.0000	$ 1.54	- 70	- 9	E	$ 8.96	+ 72	+ 9	$ 5.20	71	107	70	105
3/1	3.0000	$ .29-	-100	-13	E	$ 8.02	+ 54	+ 7	$ 6.11	91	137	90	135
4/1	4.0000	$ 2.12-	-100	-13	E	$ 7.71	+ 48	+ 6	$ 7.28	101	152	101	152
5/1	5.0000	$ 3.95-	-100	-13	E	$ 7.55	+ 45	+ 6	$ 8.45	109	164	108	162
6/1	6.0000	$ 5.78-	-100	-13	E	$ 7.46	+ 43	+ 5	$ 9.62	115	173	114	171
7/1	7.0000	$ 7.61-	-100	-13	E	$ 7.39	+ 42	+ 5	$10.79	119	179	119	179
8/1	8.0000	$ 9.44-	-100	-13	E	$ 7.35	+ 41	+ 5	$11.96	123	185	122	183
9/1	9.0000	$11.27-	-100	-13	E	$ 7.32	+ 41	+ 5	$13.13	126	189	125	188
SHORT					0-E	$ 7.08	+ 36	+ 5	$ 1.17	156	234	156	234

WHITE PASS & YUKON

	WT EXCH	MO TO EXP	FINAL EXC PR	S/E FNL	STOCK	WARRANT
	TOR	18.1	$ 30.00	.41	$ 12.25	$ 1.70

RATIO	R	A	PC	PC/MO	MAX AT	B	PC	PC/MO	BARE ACCT INVEST	MAXIMUM PROFIT ACT	ANN	PROBABLE PROFIT ACT	ANN
1/1	1.0000	$10.55	− 14	−1	E+	$999.99	+999	+999	$12.25	159	106	14	9
2/1	2.0000	$ 8.85	− 28	−2	E	$ 51.15	+318	+ 18	$12.25	173	115	28	19
3/1	3.0000	$ 7.15	− 42	−2	E	$ 41.43	+238	+ 13	$12.25	187	124	42	28
4/1	4.0000	$ 5.45	− 56	−3	E	$ 38.18	+212	+ 12	$12.25	200	133	56	37
5/1	5.0000	$ 3.75	− 69	−4	E	$ 36.56	+198	+ 11	$12.63	208	138	67	45
6/1	6.0000	$ 2.05	− 83	−5	E	$ 35.59	+191	+ 11	$13.93	201	134	73	49
7/1	7.0000	$ .35	− 97	−5	E	$ 34.94	+185	+ 10	$15.23	195	130	78	52
8/1	8.0000	$ 1.35−	−100	−6	E	$ 34.48	+181	+ 10	$16.53	190	126	82	55
9/1	9.0000	$ 3.05−	−100	−6	E	$ 34.13	+179	+ 10	$17.83	185	123	86	57
SHORT					0−E	$ 31.70	+159	+ 9	$ 1.30	131	87	131	87

Bibliography

BOOKS

Kassouf, S. T. *A Theory and an Econometric Model for Stock Purchase Warrants.* Brooklyn, N.Y.: Analytical Publishers Co., 1965.

Kassouf, S. T. *Evaluation of Convertible Securities.* Brooklyn, N.Y.: Analytical Publishers Co., 1962.

Thorp, E. O. and Kassouf, S. T. *Beat the Market—A Scientific Stock Market System.* New York: Random House, 1967.

PERIODICALS

Armstrong, Thomas H. "Stock Option Warrants," *The Analysts Journal* (May 1954).

Ayers, Herbert F. "Risk Aversion in the Warrant Markets," *Industrial Management Review,* vol. 5, no. 1 (Fall 1963).

Giguere, G. "Warrants—A Mathematical Method of Evaluation," *Analysts Journal,* vol. 14, no. 5 (November 1958).

Hallingsby, Paul Jr. "Speculative Opportunities in Stock Purchase Warrants," *Analysts Journal*, vol. 3, no. 3 (Third Quarter 1947).

Hayes, Samuel L. and Reiling, Henry B. "Sophisticated Financing Tool: The Warrant," *Harvard Business Review* (January–February 1969).

Hobbet, Richard D. "Using Stock Warrants in Corporate Acquisitions and Reorganizations," *Journal of Taxation* (March 1958).

Kassouf, S. T. "Warrant Price Behavior 1945–64," *Financial Analysts Journal* (January–February 1968).

Morrison, Russell J. "The Warrant or the Stock?" *Analysts Journal*, vol. 13, no. 5 (November 1957).

Plum, V. L. and Martin, T. J. "The Significance of Conversion Parity in Valuing Common Stock Warrants," *The Financial Review* (of the City College), vol. 1, no. 1 (February 1966).

Samuelson, Paul. "The Rational Theory of Warrant Pricing," *Industrial Management Review*, vol. 6, no. 2 (Spring 1965).

Shelton, John P. "The Relation of the Price of a Warrant to the Price of its Associated Stock," *Financial Analysts Journal* (May–June and July–August 1967, two installments).

Sprankle, Case. "Warrant Prices as Indicators of Expectations and Preferences," *Yale Economic Essays*, vol. 1, no. 2 (1961).

Turov, Daniel. "Stock or Warrant," *Barron's* (March 9, 1970).

———. "Out of the Cellar?" *Barron's* (March 27, 1972).

PRIVATE PUBLICATIONS

Barnes, Leo. *Your Investments.* New York: American Research Council, Inc., 1961.

Fried, Sidney. *The Speculative Merits of Common Stock Warrants.* New York: R.H.M. Associates, 1961.

How the Special Leverage of Warrants and Convertibles Offer You Extra Profits. Providence, R.I.: The Tillman Survey.

Leffler, George L. "Handling Stock Rights," *Pennsylvania Business Survey* (November 1957).

Schwartz, William. *Using Warrants for Leverage.* New York: Fitch Investors Service, 1957.

Warrants and the Speculator. New York: DuVal's Consensus, Inc., 1954.

Whiting, Richard. *Increase Your Profits with Warrants and Convertibles.* Garden City, N.Y.: Investing and Management Compass, Inc., 1962.

Index

A

Accounting Principles Board, 44
Accounts; *see* Brokerage account
Adjusted exercise price
  defined, 4
  dilution protection, 9–12
  stock dividends, 4, 10–12
  stock splits, 4, 10–12
  use of, 66–70
Adjusted warrant, 66–70
Adjusted warrant price, 63–64, 66–70
Advisory services, 102
After market, 117
Agau Mines, 57–58
Alleghany Corporation, 28–29, 41
American & Foreign Power Company,
  37
American Institute of Certified Public
  Accountants, 44
American Stock Exchange
  Board, 7
  warrants listed on, 39
Arbitrage, 36, 61, 71, 84–85, 94
ASE; *see* American Stock Exchange
Asked price, 18
Atlantic Richfield, 2–3
Atlas Corporation, 3, 41
A.T.&T., 17, 37, 61, 117

Authorized newspapers, 13
Avco Community Developers, 166
Avco Corporation, 37

B

Bangor Punta, 105
Barron's, 100, 118
Baruch, Bernard, 180
Bid and asked price, 18
Bond
  face value, 4
  usable, 4
Braniff Airlines, 37, 89
Brokerage account, 167–71
Buy rules, 114, 119–22
Buying on margin, 170–71

C

Call options, 19, 60
Callable warrants, 8–9, 42, 105–7
Canada Southern Petroleum, 164–65
Canadian Gas & Energy Fund Ltd., 41
Canadian warrants, 171–74
Cash account, 128, 168
Cayman Corporation, 9
Chemical Bank, 26
Chris-Craft, 135

Cities Service Company, 2
Commonwealth Edison, 9, 37, 87–89
Compound interest, 183–87
Conglomerate, 43
Congressional Life Insurance Company
    of New York, 26
Continental Telephone Corp.
    hedging with, 137–47
    leverage, 55–56
    premium, 67–70
    volatility gauge, 66
Contract writer, 19
Conversion feature; *see* Exchangeable
    warrants
Convertible bonds, 19, 45–47, 50–51
Convertible preferred stock, 19
Convertible warrants; *see* Exchange-
    able warrants
Cornering the market, 178–79
C&P Warrant Analysis, 102
Crane, Burton, 107
CTC; *see* Continental Telephone Corp.

D

Deferred exercisability, 82–83
Dilution
    defined, 9–12
    protection, 85–87, 104–5
    stock dividend, 10–12
    stock splits, 10
Dividends, 76–77, 104
Dow Jones Industrial Average, 181

E

Elgin National Industries, 67–70,
    160–61, 165
Escalation clause, 6
Exchangeable warrants
    Commonwealth Edison, 87–89
    defined, 87–89
    Warner Communications, 52–53
Ex-dividend, 82
Executive options, 20
Exercise price
    defined, 3
    dilution protection, 9–12
    escalation clause, 6

Exercise price—*Cont.*
    flush-out clause, 7
    step-down, 6
    step-ups, 6
Expiration date, 6, 74–76, 177
Expiring warrants
    buying, 103
    premium adjustment, 74–76
    reverse hedging with, 149–82
    shorting, 150–51
Extension of warrants; *see* Expiration
    date

F

Face value, bond, 4, 79–80
FED; *see* Federal Reserve Board
Federal Reserve Board
    approved list, 78–79, 127
    margin requirements, 168–71
    Regulation T, 131–32
Federal Reserve System margin re-
    quirements, 168–71
Financial Post, The, 100, 118, 172
First National Real Estate Trust, 27
First National Realty & Construction
    Corp., reverse hedging with,
    157–63
Float, 90–91
Flush-out clause, 7, 45
FNR; *see* First National Realty & Con-
    struction Corp.
Fractional shares, 5, 89–90
FRB; *see* Federal Reserve Board
FRS; *see* Federal Reserve System
Fundamental security analysis, 98
Fuqua Industries, 29

G

General Host, 135
Globe and Mail, The, 100
Good faith money, 169
Good until cancelled order, 124

H

Hedging, 130–48; *see also* Reverse
    hedging
    closing position, 147–48

Hedging—*Cont.*
identifying opportunities, 136–40
one-to-one, 133
Regulation T, 131–32
risk-reward matrix, 130
selecting ratios, 140–47
Hilton Hotel warrants, 3, 84
Houston Oils Ltd., 165
Husky Oil Ltd., 160–61

I

IBA; *see* Investment Bankers Association
Initial margin, 170–71
Installment sales, 33–34
Institutional investors, 40–41
Interest Equalization Tax, 171–73
Internal Revenue Service
Interest Equalization Tax, 171–73
tax-free exchange under, 32–33
tax-free reorganization under, 49–50
Intrinsic value, 60–63
Investment banker, 22–23
Investment Bankers Association
approaching expiration, 75–76
warrant premiums, 71–73
Investment Company of America, 41
Investors Funding Corporation, 26
IRS; *see* Internal Revenue Service
Issue price premium, 30

J–K

Jefferson Lake Petrochemicals, reverse hedging with, 154–63
JLP; *see* Jefferson Lake Petrochemicals
Kleins Department Stores, 8

L

Leasco Data Processing Equipment Corporation, 26, 37
Lectro Management, 160–61
Lerner Stores, 8
Leverage, 54–60, 65
Leverage indicator, 59, 108
Leverage ratio, 54–55

Levin-Townsend, 10–11
Ling, James, 43
Ling-Temco-Vought
hedge with, 132–35
Okonite warrant, 129
Listing, 77–79
LTV; *see* Ling-Temco-Vought

M

McCrory Corporation warrants, 7–8
Magellan Petroleum, 165
Maintenance margin, 170–71
Many-to-one reverse hedge; *see* Unbalanced reverse hedge
Mapco Corp., 88–89
Margin
initial, 170–71
maintenance, 170–71
reverse hedges, 167–71
short selling, 127–29
unlisted securities, 78
Margin account, 168
Market order, 124–25
Maximum warrant price, 62–63, 92–94
Mergers, 27
Mid-America Pipeline, 29
Millionaire, 182–83
Minimum warrant price, 62–63, 92–94
Mohawk Data Sciences, 89
Molybdenum Corp., 178–79
Moody's Industrial's, 99
Multiple regression analysis, 94–97

N

NASD; *see* National Association of Security Dealers
National Association of Securities Dealers, 17, 77–78
National Quotation Bureau
over-the-counter trading, 15–17
pink sheets, 15–17
Negative intrinsic value, 60–61, 64
New issues, buying of, 116–19
New York Stock Exchange
listing of warrants, 18, 39
margin requirements, 169–71

Nondetachability, 82–83
Nonexercisability, 82–83
Nonprofessional, 9
Nontransferability, 82–83
Norm price, 94–97, 112–14
Norm price curves, 96
Normalized warrant; *see* Adjusted warrant
NYSE; *see* New York Stock Exchange

O

One-to-one reverse hedge, 151–53
Orders
  good until cancelled, 124
  market, 124–25
  stop loss, 124
Original financing, 23–24
OTC; *see* Over-the-counter
Over-the-counter, 15–17, 39–40, 77–79

P

Package, 15–17
P/E; see Price-earnings ratio
Percent premium, 64
Perpetual warrants, 5, 41
Pink sheets, 15–17, 106
Plus cash convertibles, 21
Preemptive right, 19
Preliminary prospectus, 101
Premium, 63–65, 109–12
Present value
  tables, 184, 186
  theory, 183–87
Price determination, 71–97
Price-earnings ratio, 73–74, 91–92
Private placements, 37
Professional, 9
Promoters, 24, 51–52
Prospectus, 101
Put-and-call broker, 19

Q–R

Qualified stock option plan, 52
RCA, 130
Real Estate Investment Trusts, 119

Red herring, 101
Redeemable bonds, 79–80
Registration with Securities and Exchange Commission; *see* Securities and Exchange Commission
Regulation T, 131–32, 143
Relative stock price, 67
Relative warrant; *see* Adjusted warrant
Relative warrant price, 67
Reorganizations, 27–29
Research vehicles, 99–102, 118
Residual value, 9
Reverse hedging, 149–82; *see also* Hedging
  Canadian warrants, 171–74
  case for, 180–82
  choosing the mix, 160–67
  defined, 149–50
  identifying candidates, 159–60
  long warrants, 179–80
  one-to-one ratio, 151–53
  potential pitfalls, 177–79
  selling short expiring warrants, 150–51
  timing, 174–77
  unbalanced ratio, 153–59
  use of margin, 167–71
Rights, 19
Risk-reward matrix, 130
Rockwood Computer, 10–11

S

S/E; *see* Relative stock price
SEC; *see* Securities and Exchange Commission
Securities and Exchange Commission
  Daily News Digest, 101, 118
  library, 118
  red herring, 101
  registration with, 99
  warrant agreement, 12, 23
Security analysis, 98
Sell rules, 114–16, 119–22
Senior securities, 4, 15
Short account, 168
Short selling, 123–30
  borrowing for, 127–29
  margin requirements, 127–28

Short selling—*Cont.*
  Regulation T, 131–32
  reverse hedges, 167–71
  shorting power, 134
  squeeze, 178–79
Short squeeze, 178–79
Shorting power, 134
Specialist's book, 124
Spreads, 90–91
Standard & Poor's Corporation
  Daily News, 100
  Dividend Record, 101
  Standard Corporation Records, 99, 118
Step-down, 6
Step-ups, 6, 81–82, 103
Stock dividends, 4
Stock splits, 4
Stokely-Van Camp, Inc., 41
Stop loss order, 124–25
Street name, 168
Subscription price, 19
Sweetener, 29–30
Symington-Wayne, 27

T

Tax-free reorganization, 49–50
Tender offer, 24–27
Tenneco, Inc., 29
Texas International Airlines, 41
Thin market, 90–91
TOR; *see* Toronto Stock Exchange
Toronto Stock Exchange
  Jefferson Lake short position, 154–55
  margin requirements, 169–71
  member firms, 172–73
Trading on the equity, 44–45
Trans World Airlines, 3, 84–85
Transfer agent, 3, 12
Treasury stock, 1
Tri-Continental Corporation, 2, 41, 56–57, 59–60

U

Unbalanced reverse hedge, 153–59
Underwriters, 24

Underwriter's fee, 22–23, 51–52
Unit, 15–17, 23, 40, 48–49
United Canso Oil & Gas, 160–61, 166
United National Investors Corporation, 27
United Utilities Corp., 37
Usable bonds, 4, 79–80

V

Value Line Convertible Survey, The, 102
Volatility, 65–66, 80–81
Volatility gauge, 66
Voting rights, 13

W–Z

W/E; see Relative warrant price
Wall Street Journal, 100, 118
Warner Communications, 21, 52–53, 87–89
Warrant
  acceptance of, 34–39
  adjusted exercise price, 4
  advisory services, 102
  agent, 12
  agreement, 12–13, 177
  call on other than common, 83–85
  callable, 8–9
  Canadian, 171–74
  certificate, 13
  changes in terms: price and time, 6
  conversion feature, 87–89
  convertible, 87–89
  creation of,
    acquisitions, 24–27
    mergers, 27
    original financing, 23–24
    reorganizations, 27–29
    tender offer, 24–27
  deferred exercisability, 82–83
  defined life, 5, 109
  definition of, 1–11
  dilution, 9–12
  dilution protection, 85–87, 104–5
  distinguished from other convertibles, 19–21
  dividends, 29, 104
  effect of prime interest rate, 42–43

Warrant—*Cont.*

employee option plan with, 52
escalation clause, 6
exchangeable, 87–89
exercise of, 36, 45–46
exercise price, 3
expiration date, 6, 74–76, 109, 177
extended life, 7
float, 90–91
flush-out clause, 7, 45
fractional shares, 5
future uses, 51–53
growth in issuance, 42
hedge, 130–48
historical use, 36
institutional investment in, 40–41
intrinsic value, 60–63
leverage with, 54–60
leverage indicator, 59
leverage ratio, 54–55
limited security, 13–15
listing of, 77–79
marketability, 39
maximum and minimum price of, 62–63, 92–94
nondetachability, 82–83
nonexercisability, 82–83
nontransferability, 82–83
norm price, 94–97

Warrant—*Cont.*

perpetual, 5, 41
premium, 63–65
private placements, 37
reasons for use, 29–36
residual value, 9
reverse hedge, 149–82
specified time, 5
step-down, 6
step-ups, 6, 81–82, 103
supply and demand, 90–91
tax benefits to issuer, 30–34
thin market in, 90–91
traded, 15–19
    ask price, 18
    bid price, 18
    cum, 15–17
    ex, 15–17
    one-to-one basis, 17–18
    package, 15–17
    unit, 15–17, 23, 40, 48–49
    WD, 15–17
    WI, 15–17
    XW, 15–17
usable bonds, 4, 79–80
volatility of, 65–66, 80–81
When detached, 15–17
White Pass & Yukon, 165
Zayre Corp., 37

This book has been set in 12 and 10 point Bodoni Book, leaded 3 points. Chapter numbers are 48 point Twentieth Century Light; chapter titles are 24 point Twentieth Century Light. The size of the type page is 24 by 44 picas.